PROGRAM GUIDE

W9-AHF-374

Stress Management
for Adolescents

A Cognitive-Behavioral Program

Diane de Anda

Research Press
2612 North Mattis Avenue, Champaign, Illinois 61822
(800) 519-2707 www.researchpress.com

Composition by Jeff Helgesen

Cover design by Linda Brown, Positive I.D. Graphic Design

Printed by Malloy, Inc.

ISBN 0–87822–444–0 (Program Guide and Audio CD)

ISBN 0–87822–483–1 (Program Guide)

Library of Congress Control Number 2001096574

Contents

Program Overview

Young people experience stress from a variety of sources: school, parents, friends and peers—even themselves, in the form of their own desires, goals, and expectations. Many have tried different ways of dealing with stress but have not been successful doing so. Although no one can make the world stress-free, students can learn effective techniques for reducing stress and handling stressful situations. This program is designed to help students of middle and high school age cope more effectively with the multiple stressors in their lives.

The aim of the program is to effect both cognitive and behavioral changes. That is, it offers both knowledge and specific coping techniques to expand students' behavioral repertoires. In particular, the program includes information and activities to help students achieve the following objectives:

1. Understand the nature of stress and its impact on health and behavior.
2. Recognize the stressors and signs of stress in their own lives.
3. Recognize the cognitive components of stress, especially the effects of one's automatic thoughts and internal dialogue on appraisal of stressors.
4. Learn various relaxation methods to reduce muscle tension related to stress.
5. Learn cognitive techniques to increase accurate appraisal of stressors.
6. Learn specific behavioral techniques for reducing the degree of stress and distress.
7. Learn a problem-solving strategy for dealing with situations that are stressors or potential stressors.
8. Integrate cognitive and behavioral coping strategies in their daily lives.

PROGRAM MATERIALS

Program Guide

Useful for either whole-class or small-group instruction, this Program Guide describes a preliminary session for pretesting, ten content-based sessions, and a final session consisting of review of major concepts and the administration posttest measures. Every session begins with an outline of the session's agenda, a list of materials needed, and a list of session objectives written to reflect the specific skills or knowledge to be gained by participants. Sessions include a full script and instructions to the leader, student forms and worksheets, and visual aids.

Instructions to the leader appear in italic type; text not in italics indicates what the leader might say while conducting the session. Although it is a good idea to stay as close to the script as possible to avoid omitting important concepts or instructions, it is neither necessary nor desirable to follow the script word for word. The teaching should be interactive so students feel they are participating in the process rather than passively absorbing information.

A variety of instructional methods are employed: didactic instruction, group process, individual and group activities (written exercises, role playing, etc.), and specific relaxation and coping strategies. The relaxation and coping strategies are practiced in the group session and reinforced by home practice assignments. Motivational activities conducted during the session are an important part of the program because they reinforce the learning of specific concepts via an attention-grabbing, entertaining interactive process, thereby capturing and maintaining students' interest.

Supplementary materials relating to session content and program evaluation are given in four appendixes.

Appendix A: Relaxation Scripts

This appendix gives the full text of Scanning Relaxation, as recorded in the audio CD accompanying this program. It also includes the script for Quick Body Scanning, a briefer process that students may use any time during the day, both in and out of school.

Appendix B: Program Forms

Program Forms include rating sheets and worksheets used throughout the program. These may be photocopied and distributed to students as needed at each session, or they may be made available for students to pick up at a central location.

Appendix C: Figures

Figures consist of visual displays of important vocabulary and concepts. Referenced in the text to reinforce students' learning, they may be reproduced in any whole-class format (on a chalkboard or easel pad, on an overhead projector, etc.).

Appendix D: Program Evaluation Measures

This appendix includes three measures that may be used as both pretests and posttests, and others that may be used as additional posttests and measures of student progress.

Student Manual

The Student Manual accompanying this Program Guide gives participants the opportunity to follow along with the leader's presentation of major concepts and activities. It offers motivational activities, written and role-play exercises, written examples and diagrams of major concepts, and narrative examples of stressful situations commonly faced by middle and high school students. The Student Manual provides a reference students can use during sessions, consult outside the sessions, and refer to after the program is over.

Audio CD

As noted, an audio CD included with the program gives the text of the Scanning Relaxation procedure, a thirteen-minute exercise in systematically relaxing various muscle groups. Each session includes Scanning Relaxation practice, and students are asked to practice on their own at home with their own copy of the CD. Although it is possible to conduct the program without each participant's having a CD, the prompts and review of the process on the CD make using and learning the procedure much easier.

RELAXATION AND COPING TECHNIQUES

The program presents four main relaxation and coping techniques:

1. *Calm Body.* The Scanning Relaxation and Quick Body Scanning procedures for reducing muscle tension across all major muscle groups
2. *Clear Mind.* Cognitive coping procedures, which involve accurately appraising the facts and meaning attributed to stressors
3. *Calming Actions.* Behavioral coping procedures, including letting out feelings, talking with others about feelings, employing exercise and rest, and using distraction
4. *Problem-Solving Actions.* A problem-solving procedure to deal with stressors by identifying the problem, selecting a goal, generating alternative solutions, determining the consequences of each solution, and rating solutions on the basis of predicted consequences

An abbreviated relaxation process, differential relaxation, is also described for eliminating tension in specific muscle groups.

THEORETICAL FOUNDATION

This stress management program integrates a number of theoretical principles and clinical and research findings in a group learning process geared to the abilities and interests of adolescent populations. Specifically, the program is based on cognitive-behavioral principles derived from the theory, research, and clinical models of such proponents as Aaron Beck, Albert Bandura, Arnold Lazarus, and Donald Meichenbaum. The psychobiological model of stress is also incorporated, particularly the concepts of Hans Selye. The Scanning Relaxation and Quick Body Scanning procedures are adapted from the work of Edward H. Charlesworth and Ronald G. Nathan (1982).

In the program, stress is conceptualized as a psychobiological response based on the appraisal of threat or danger to one's personal domain. According to Beck (1976), each individual's personal domain varies, encompassing a broad range of areas valued by the person, beginning with his or her life, well-being, and self-esteem and extending to persons, objects, or even abstract concepts (e.g., loyalty, fidelity, patriotism). In Beck's model, this appraisal or cognition determines the individual's physiological response, affect, and behavioral inclination. This relationship is illustrated in the following figure.

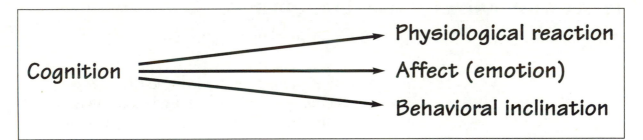

If the cognition is one of threat or danger, this will result in various physiological reactions such as tachycardia, perspiring palms, muscle tension, and the like; an affect of fear or anxiety (stress); and a behavioral inclination to flee or fight. A change in the cognition—that is, the appraisal of the situation—will result in a change in the other three responses. For example, if upon closer examination a person discovers that the object appraised as a danger is really *not* a rattlesnake but a rope, this change in cognition will result in a change in physiological reaction (lowered heart rate, lessening of muscle tension, etc.), affect (calm), and behavioral inclination (to approach rather than flee).

The Clear Mind technique developed for this program is based on this model in that students are taught to appraise the stressor accurately so that stress in its physiological, affective, and behavioral manifestations is reduced in response to situations that pose little or no danger to the personal domain. First, students are taught to assess the *facts* of a situation to avoid misperception and errors in judgment. Second, they uncover the *meaning* they attribute to the situation and learn to explore alternative explanations or meanings. For example, a student may learn that any difference in opinion with a friend produces high levels of stress because the meaning he or she ascribes to the disagreement is one of total rejection and loss of the friendship. In many instances, the Clear Mind technique is helpful in correcting cognitive distortions that lead to stress.

As the following figure shows, Arnold Lazarus's (Lazarus, 1997; Lazarus & Folkman, 1984) model links the appraisal process to the coping actions undertaken in response.

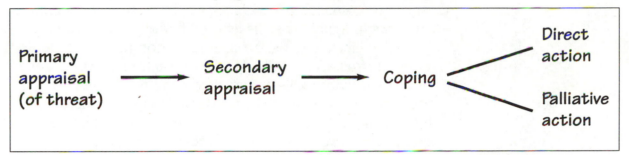

Primary appraisal refers to the assessment of the threat value of the situation. *Secondary appraisal* refers to an evaluation of the ability to cope with the situation and the consequences that will result from attempting to cope with it. Coping responses are of two kinds: direct action, or action taken to handle or change the external situation (e.g., fight, flight), and palliative action, or action taken to alter one's internal response to the situation (e.g., relaxation, use of drugs/alcohol, cognitive control). A stress management program requires components that deal with cognitive control to assure an accurate appraisal process and the expansion of the individual's coping repertoire, in terms of both direct and palliative action.

Emphasis is placed on the palliative-coping techniques of Scanning Relaxation and Quick Body Scanning to reduce muscle tension associated with stress. These techniques are elicited by the cue "Calm Body." Other means of palliative coping, called "Calming Actions," are briefly presented. These include expressing ("letting out") one's feelings, talking with someone about one's feelings, exercise, rest, and the use of distraction. A brief problem-solving process is taught as a direct-action coping strategy.

The program employs the three main components that Meichenbaum (1977, 1985, 1993) has found to be successful in his stress inoculation treatment for anxiety: (a) reducing physiological arousal, (b) changing what the person says to himself or herself about the situation, and (c) employing specific coping behaviors.

This program is also designed to enhance each student's sense of self-efficacy—that is, the belief that he or she can "organize and execute courses of action required to manage prospective situations" (Bandura, 1995, p. 2). This sense of self-efficacy is necessary if the skills learned in the program are to be generalized to the student's everyday life: "Efficacy beliefs influence how people think, feel, motivate themselves, and act" (p. 3).

The program incorporates all four of the methods that Bandura indicates are involved in developing a strong sense of self-efficacy.

1. *Mastery experiences.* The home practice assignments require students to apply the skills learned in the group session to everyday life situations. Arousal-reduction techniques, cognitive restructuring methods, calming action strategies, and problem-solving skills are practiced and reinforced. To increase the likelihood of success (mastery) outside the classroom, the assignments are incremental and subsequent to practicing the skills in the group session.

2. *Vicarious experiences.* Modeling of skills and noting the successful implementation of these skills by peers "raises the observers' beliefs that they, too, possess the capabilities to master comparable activities" (Bandura, 1995, p. 3). Group discussions that focus on peer application of the program's concepts and skills enhance the learning process.

3. *Social persuasion.* The entire program is an argument for the individual's ability to exert both self-control and external control (control over his or her environment). Each student is given the opportunity to test this assertion in exercises that demonstrate and reinforce this position.

4. *Enhancement of physical status.* As Bandura notes, "People rely partly on their physiological and emotional states in judging their capabilities" (p. 4). The program teaches students methods for controlling physiological arousal (the Calm Body technique) and cognitive restructuring for changing their affective states (the Clear Mind technique).

PROGRAM EVALUATION

Process measures are included for assessing the effectiveness of the various coping techniques. Outcome measures, in the form of pretests and posttests, evaluate level of stress, ability to handle stress, frequency and effectiveness of various coping strategies, and knowledge of the program's major concepts.

Appendix D offers a number of evaluation instruments from which you can choose to determine the progress of participants and the effectiveness of the program. The appendix offers brief guidelines for using these measures.

SOME FINAL CONSIDERATIONS

Even though program concepts have been simplified and are illustrated by multiple examples, it is important to remember that students assimilate and generalize concepts and skills at different rates. For some students, additional examples may be necessary, and others may have difficulty applying the concepts from the examples given to their own problems.

Individual assistance and the frequent use of student examples in the group may facilitate learning. Take care, however, to warn students not to give examples that are too personal, and remind them that they are to maintain confidentiality outside of the group. An agreement students sign at the beginning of the program clearly states the need for confidentiality. If a student does bring up a very personal situation, be sure to intervene and protect the student; if it is too late to intervene, stress confidentiality and normalize the student's situation.

Almost without exception, students respond positively to the stress management approaches. However, sometimes a student who has used a technique incorrectly will report feeling no stress reduction—for example, no reduction in body tension after practicing Scanning Relaxation. In this case, it is important to troubleshoot the problem. If you ask the student to explain how he or she used the technique, you will likely uncover a reason for the lack of success. Practicing Scanning Relaxation in a room where people are talking (or even arguing), for example, is unlikely to result in much reduction of body tension. People are also quite individual in what stress reduction techniques work best for them. For example, crying might make one student feel a release of tension, but it may actually make another student feel worse. The program includes a wide range of techniques: If one technique does not work for a student, you can suggest that the student choose another one.

Even though students may be dealing with difficult situations, it is important to maintain a positive and upbeat atmosphere. The learning process should be enjoyable for both the learners and the instructor. Students' participation, creativity, and generalization to their own experiences should be encouraged.

REFERENCES AND SELECTED READINGS

Bandura, A. (Ed.). (1995). *Self-efficacy in changing societies.* New York: Cambridge University Press.

Beck, A. T. (1976). *Cognitive therapy and the emotional disorders.* New York: International Universities Press.

Beck, A. T., & Weisharr, M. (1989). Cognitive therapy. In A. Freeman, K. M. Simon, & L. E. Arkowitz (Eds.), *Comprehensive handbook of cognitive therapy.* New York: Plenum.

Beck, J. S. (1995). *Cognitive therapy: Basics and beyond.* New York: Guilford.

Charlesworth, E. A., & Nathan, R. G. (1984). *Stress management: A comprehensive guide to wellness.* New York: Ballantine.

Clark, D. A., & Beck, A. T. (1990). Cognitive therapy of anxiety and depression. In R. E. Ingram (Ed.), *Contemporary psychological approaches to depression: Theory, research, and treatment.* New York: Plenum.

Emery, G. (1993). Radical cognitive therapy. In K. T. Kuehlwein & H. Rosen (Eds.), *Cognitive therapies in action: Evolving innovative practices.* San Francisco: Jossey-Bass.

Lazarus, A. (1997). *Brief but comprehensive psychotherapy.* New York: Springer.

Lazarus, A., & Folkman, S. (1984). *Stress appraisal and coping.* New York: Springer.

Meichenbaum, D. (1977). *Cognitive-behavior modification.* New York: Plenum.

Meichenbaum, D. (1985). *Stress inoculation training.* New York: Pergamon.

Meichenbaum, D. (1993). A constructivist narrative perspective on stress and coping: Stress inoculation applications. In L. Goldberger & S. Breznitz (Eds.), *Handbook of stress: Theoretical and clinical aspects.* New York: Free Press.

Monat, A., & Lazarus, R. S. (Eds.). (1991). *Stress and coping: An anthology* (3rd ed.). New York: Columbia University Press

Selye, H. (1956). *The stress of life.* New York: McGraw-Hill.

Selye, H. (1974). *Stress without distress.* New York: Lippincott.

Pretesting and Program Orientation

Before beginning the content sessions, meet with the group to administer pretest measures. It is important to conduct pretesting *before* the first session; otherwise, the session will be too long. Three measures that can be used for pretesting appear in Appendix D of this guide, along with descriptions of these measures and guidelines for using them.

In this preliminary meeting, you will also want to give students a brief orientation to the program and its goals. Greet the group, indicating that today is the beginning of a process that will span eleven sessions. Indicate that they will be learning and trying out (both in the group and on their own in their everyday world) all kinds of new techniques for reducing their stress.

Cover the following points, then give students a chance to ask any questions:

1. You recognize the amount of stress they experience from a variety of sources: school, parents, friends and peers, themselves (e.g., their own desires, goals, and expectations).

2. You know that they have tried different ways of dealing with stress but that they have not always been successful in doing so.

3. No one can make the world stress-free, but they can learn techniques for reducing stress and handling stressful situations.

4. The program will involve learning both new ways of *thinking* and specific *actions* they can use to reduce the stress in their lives.

5. Using these techniques, they will be able to deal with stressful situations more comfortably and effectively. This should lead to better functioning in general in their world as well as to better mental and physical health.

SESSION 1

Identifying Stress

AGENDA

1. Introduction
2. Stress Management Program Agreement
3. What is stress? (Motivational Activity)
   Labeling stress
   Signs of stress (behavioral and physiological)
   Stressors
4. Muscle tension and stress (Motivational Activity)
5. Practice session: Muscle tensing and relaxing
6. Preparing for Scanning Relaxation
   Scanning Relaxation Rating Sheets
   Slow breathing
   Getting settled
   Total body tension
7. Scanning Relaxation
8. Home practice: *Daily Scanning Relaxation*

MATERIALS

➤ Student Manuals (one for each student)
➤ Figures 1 and 2 (reproduced in a whole-class format)
➤ Name tags and pens
➤ A balloon and a straight pin
➤ Scanning Relaxation CD and CD player
➤ A Scanning Relaxation CD for each student
➤ Scanning Relaxation Rating Sheets (several copies for each student)

OBJECTIVES

Students will . . .

1. Understand and sign the Stress Management Program Agreement.
2. Learn a variety of labels for stress (including their own).

3. Recognize behavioral and physiological signs of stress (including their own).

4. Understand that stress is a part of everyday life and be able to recognize when it is functional and appropriate.

5. Be able to identify internal and external stressors.

6. Understand the effects of muscle tension and relaxation on health and well-being.

7. Practice Scanning Relaxation.

PROCEDURE

Introduction

*Welcome the students to the first session, and distribute the Student Manuals, one per participant. (You can paraphrase the welcome on **page 1** if you wish.) Tell the group they will be using the manuals during each session and after the sessions to review what they learn on their own.*

Next pass out the name tags and pens, and have students write their names and put on the tags. In round-robin fashion, have students give their names and say one thing they would like to get out of the group.

Stress Management Program Agreement

*Refer the group to the Stress Management Program Agreement on **page 2** of their manuals. Go over the purpose of the program, the main learning tasks, rules for group participation, and expectations. Have each student sign and date the agreement. Indicate the schedule for future sessions, and discuss any other necessary details.*

What Is Stress?

Display Figure 1 in a whole-class format.

STRESS

Figure 1

Motivational Activity To help us understand what stress is and how it makes us feel, let's start with an imaginary situation: Imagine that everyone in your school and everyone in your rival school are all sitting in the stands of *(name a local sports arena)*. A millionaire has decided to give one school $100,000 and the other $1,000. He has put every student's name into a computer to select a student who will help decide what amount each school gets.

The millionaire comes up on the stage in the middle of the arena and pushes the "enter" button on the computer. The computer makes a whirring noise as it goes through the thousands of names. Suddenly, the scoreboard lights up with gold and silver stars and exploding fireworks, and your name appears in huge flashing letters. Your principal takes the microphone and asks you to come down on the stage. At first you can't even stand up, but your friends push and tug until they get you moving down the aisle.

The whole arena is thundering with the sounds of all the students in your school cheering and stomping their feet, and all the students in the other school booing and hissing as the spotlight follows you up onto the center of the stage. The millionaire steps forward and tells everyone to be quiet. Suddenly, the huge arena becomes silent as 10,000 eyes are staring at you, standing in the spotlight.

The millionaire leads you over to the computer and puts your hand on the computer mouse. A giant maze appears on the scoreboard above you. The millionaire gives the following instructions:

> You have one minute to use the computer mouse to get through the maze on the screen. When you reach the end of the maze, you will see two doors. Each is the door to a treasure room; one room has $100,000 in treasure, the other $1,000. Whichever room you choose is the amount your school wins; the amount in the other treasure room goes to your rival school. If you don't make your decision in sixty seconds, both schools lose.

Then he says, "Get ready." Sixty seconds appear at the top of the scoreboard. You adjust your hand on the mouse and move it to the center of the mousepad.

He says, "Set." You look up at the scoreboard and see the icon you'll be leading through the maze.

"Go." The seconds remaining changes to fifty-nine, and the countdown begins.

You speed your icon around corners and down long corridors. You wiggle it through winding passages. The seconds are ticking away. You bang into a dead end; quickly, you turn around and weave back to the entrance and try another route. You weave around the maze faster and faster as the seconds are counting off.

Finally, with ten seconds left on the clock, you get to the end of the maze and face the two doors. The seconds are racing by on the scoreboard. You need to make a decision: door one or door two. Thousands of voices are yelling, "Choose, choose, choose, choose!" The scoreboard flashes: seven seconds, six seconds, five seconds, four seconds, three seconds, two seconds, one second. . . . How do you feel?

To stimulate interest and personalize the experience of stress, have students describe their stress reactions (emotions, physiological and behavioral reactions, and so forth).

Labeling Stress

What is stress? People have lots of different labels for stress. Look at **page 3** in your manuals. Some people say, "I feel really stressed out" or "I feel really tense" or "I feel nervous" or "I feel upset."

Which of these words do you use? Are there other words you use to describe these feelings? If so, write them on the blank lines.

Discuss responses and make note of the most common terms and any new terms.

We use these words to describe things we're experiencing, our feelings, and even some of the things we're thinking about.

Signs of Stress

Turn to **page 4** in your manuals. When we say we're tense or upset, often we show it in ways other people can notice. We call these **SIGNS OF STRESS.**

Tell students you will demonstrate some of these signs. Demonstrate various different stress behaviors—for instance, pacing, drumming fingers, biting nails, fidgeting, tapping your foot, and twirling a strand of hair. After each one, ask the group to identify the sign of stress.

These signs of stress are things we *do* that show we are tense or upset. These are called **BEHAVIORAL SIGNS OF STRESS.** Each person has his or her own behavioral signs of stress.

On **page 4,** list some things people might notice you doing when you feel tense or upset.

After students have had a chance to write, have them briefly share (verbally and/or via demonstration) their signs of stress with the group. If they are hesitant, begin by sharing a way you show stress.

Important things are also happening inside us that other people don't know about when we are tense or upset. These private signs of stress are often the ones that bother us the most.

Some examples might be that your stomach gets upset or feels like it's burning, or the palms of your hands get wet and clammy. Or maybe you feel like crying, but you bite down on your jaw really hard and hold back the tears. We call these the **PHYSIOLOGICAL (BODY) SIGNS OF STRESS.**

*Encourage students to list, on the remaining spaces on **page 4,** some of the ways they feel inside when they are tense, stressed, or upset. After students have finished, begin by sharing a physiological sign of your own, then encourage students to do the same.*

Let's look at the next two pages in the manual and discuss all the different ways our bodies show signs of stress.

*Discuss the behavioral signs of stress shown in the drawings on **page 5,** and ask students to name some of their own behavioral signs.*

*Next, go over **page 6,** on physiological signs of stress. Ask students to circle the physiological signs they have and add any others they have that do not appear in the drawing.*

Stressors

These pages include many of the signs people show when they are feeling stressed. But how do these different signs develop?

To answer this question, let's go back to our original question, "What is stress?" According to a famous doctor and scientist named Hans Selye, stress is a necessary part of everyday life. All stress is *not* bad.

*Refer students to **page 7** in their manuals. Read and discuss the two examples in which stress is positive (shivering and perspiring, being chased by a tiger).*

Display Figure 2 in a whole-class format.

STRESSORS

Figure 2

The cold, the heat, and the tiger are **STRESSORS.** Because they are outside of you, these are examples of **EXTERNAL STRESSORS.** On the lines provided, list three of your own external stressors. These could be people, situations, or places.

Encourage students to list external stressors, then share examples. Sample answers include a growling dog, a teacher's announcing a pop quiz, and having to give a speech in front of the class. Be sure to respect privacy by suggesting that students share only examples they feel are appropriate for group discussion.

There are also **INTERNAL STRESSORS,** or stressors inside you. For example, suppose you think about an exam, your heart begins to pound, and you feel sick to your stomach.

In this situation, what is the stressor? *(your thoughts)* What are the signs of stress? *(pounding heart, upset stomach)* What kind of signs of stress are these? *(body, physiological)*

On the last two lines of **page 7**, write any internal stressors you may have experienced. These would be specific thoughts or mental images (pictures) that upset you.

Allow students to share. Sample answers include the following.

➤ Picturing the class laughing at you when you give a speech

➤ Thinking you may have missed your bus

➤ Thinking the elevator you're in might get stuck

Muscle Tension and Stress

Motivational Activity   One way we often react to a stressor is by tensing our muscles. Let's look at this balloon to get an idea of what we mean by tense muscles. A deflated balloon can be stretched and pulled easily. *(Demonstrate with the balloon.)* But let's look at a blown-up balloon. *(Blow up the balloon.)*

Now that the same balloon is tight, it can't be moved much at all—not without the danger of popping it. This is similar to when your muscles are tight and tense. You can't "pop" them, but they feel tight and are uncomfortable or painful to move.

Now let's say that your little brother or sister has this balloon and wants to play a trick on you. He or she might sneak up behind you and pop it like this. *(Show everyone the pin, then pop the balloon.)*

How does your body react? *(Let students answer.)* Right, you'd be startled. You might jump, your heart might beat faster, and you might feel all your muscles tighten up. These are good, normal, healthy reactions—built into human beings to help us survive. As soon as we see that it is just a trick and there is no danger, our bodies begin to calm down and relax again.

We have a problem, however, if our bodies startle and get rigid very often or if we often react to the events and people around us by tensing and tightening our muscles. Over time, our muscles can tighten up to an extreme, so we look like tin soldiers. *(Demonstrate by showing a rigid walk.)*

But muscle tenseness can also be more subtle: Muscles might tighten up just a little bit, or only certain muscles might tighten up. Sometimes we get used to this level of muscle tension so we don't even notice it until after a while, when we have physical symptoms:

➤ Headaches

➤ Cramps in various parts of our bodies

➤ A stiff, tight jaw

➤ Tight, painful muscles across the shoulders or neck

You also become tired more quickly than usual—the reason is that your muscles have been working hard all day! Think how you'd feel at the end of the day if you had walked like a tin soldier all day long. *(Demonstrate the tin-soldier walk again.)*

Practice Session: Muscle Tensing and Relaxing

Keeping your muscles relaxed is one way to let go of stress in the body. We are going to do an exercise that will teach us to relax different parts of our bodies so we can relax tense muscles whenever we want. This will help us lead healthier and less stressful lives.

The first step in learning to relax our muscles is to be sure we understand how our muscles *feel* when they are relaxed.

To know for sure, we will first tense a muscle area—for instance, by making a fist *(demonstrate)*—and see how it feels when it's all tensed up, then release the tension in that muscle area—by opening and relaxing the hand *(demonstrate)*.

By doing this, we can see how tight, tense muscles and comfortable, relaxed muscles feel different. You try it now, beginning with your hand.

Hand

(Lead the group in making a fist.) Feel how tight and pulled the muscles feel. Now open and let your hand relax and go limp. Notice how comfortable the muscles in your hand now feel.

Shoulders

Next I want you to pull up your shoulders as high as you can, like this. *(Demonstrate pulling up your shoulders toward your ears.)* Now let your shoulders drop down. Notice how they feel when they are relaxed.

Head and face

Wrinkle up your forehead. Do you feel the tension? Now relax and let go. Try to smooth out your forehead. Notice the difference.

Squint your eyes as tightly as you can. Feel the tension around your eyes. Now say to yourself, "Relax and let go," and feel the difference as you relax the muscles around your eyes.

Mouth and jaws

Make a forced smile with your mouth. Your upper and lower lips and both of your cheeks should feel tense. Your lips should be pulled hard against your teeth. Now relax the muscles on each side of your mouth and notice the feeling when those muscles loosen.

Now clench your jaws tightly. Feel the tension in your jaw muscles. Now say, "Relax and let go," and notice the difference.

Neck

Tilt your head forward until your chin touches your chest. Feel the tension in the front of your neck, but especially in the back of your neck. Gradually put your head back into an upright position. Notice how relaxed and comfortable the front and back neck muscles feel.

Now put your head way back, as far as it will go, so you feel tension in the back of your neck, but especially in the front of your neck. Notice where it is especially tense.

Put your head back into an upright position, and notice the difference.

Arms

Bend your arms toward your shoulders, and double them up as you would to show off your biceps muscles. Feel the tension. Now say, "Relax and let go," and feel the difference.

Back

Slide forward in your chair. Push your elbows towards each other behind your back. Notice that your shoulders and the middle of your back feel pulled and tight.

Gradually relax by moving back into the chair while you straighten out your arms and put them on your lap in a relaxed position. Notice the feeling as those muscles loosen, switching from tension to relaxation, and then fully relax. Notice the difference in the way the muscles feel. Now say, "Relax and let go."

Stomach

Now tighten the muscles in your stomach area. Feel the tension. Now say, "Relax and let go," and notice the difference.

Legs

Lift your legs, and bend your toes right up toward your knees. Feel the tension. Try to touch your knees with your toes. Feel the tension in your lower legs. Now say, "Relax and let go," and feel the tension slip away.

Preparing for Scanning Relaxation

Scanning Relaxation Rating Sheets

Now that we've practiced tensing and relaxing our muscles, we're almost ready to do the complete Scanning Relaxation exercise.

Before we begin, we need to fill out a form that will help us compare how our bodies feel before and after our relaxation exercise. Turn to **page 8** in your manuals.

Refer to the Scanning Relaxation Rating Sheet. Read the directions aloud, and have everyone fill the sheet out, including yourself.

Slow Breathing

During the Scanning Relaxation exercise, you will be asked to breathe slowly to help you relax. Let's talk briefly about how that works.

When you're upset, your breathing becomes shallow and speeds up faster than normal. When you're relaxed, your breathing is slower, deeper, and more even.

Slow, deep breathing helps your muscles relax and get more oxygen. Slow breathing also sends a message to your body that it's time to relax and get comfortable.

Slow breathing is an important part of our relaxation exercise. Throughout the exercise, you will be asked to inhale *slowly,* then exhale and say to yourself, "Relax and let go."

These breaths should be slow, gentle, normal breaths, not deep gasps, so you don't hyperventilate. If you feel short of breath at any time, tell me.

Slow breathing should make you feel more relaxed when it's done correctly. As we go through the exercise, you will feel more and more comfortable.

Getting Settled

Dim the lights, pull down the shades, and tell students to close their eyes.

First, let's get settled and ready for the Scanning Relaxation exercise. Spend a little time getting as comfortable as you can. While you are finding a good sitting position, you will also want to loosen any tight clothing. Your legs and arms should be slightly apart.

Now we're ready to begin.

Total Body Tension

First, tense every muscle in your body. Tense your jaws, eyes, arms, hands, chest, back, stomach, legs, and feet, as we did during our practice session, but now tense all of them at the same time. Feel the tension all over your body.

Hold the tension briefly, then silently say, "Relax and let go," as you breathe out . . . let your whole body relax . . . feel the wave of calm come over you as you stop tensing. Feel the relief.

Gently close your eyes, and take another deep breath . . . study the tension as you hold your breath . . . slowly breathe out, and silently say, "Relax and let go." Feel the relaxation deepen.

Scanning Relaxation

Now I'm going to play a CD with some instructions for scanning your body and letting go of muscle tension. Whenever you feel upset and sense your muscles getting tense, you can scan them, then "relax and let go."

At the end of the session I will give each of you a copy of the CD so you can practice this relaxation exercise at home.

Play the CD. (The script for the Scanning Relaxation exercise appears in Appendix A.)

*After the exercise is over, instruct students to fill out the after-practice Scanning Relaxation Rating Sheet on **page 9** in their manuals. Discuss any differences between the before- and after-practice sheets.*

Home Practice

*Pass out the CDs, one per student. Tell students to turn to **page 10** in their manuals, then explain the home practice assignment.*

I would like you to use the CD to practice the Scanning Relaxation exercise at least once a day between now and the time we meet for the next session.

➤ Choose a quiet place.

➤ Dim the lights if possible.

➤ Wear loose, comfortable clothing.

➤ Practice in a comfortable place. A lounge chair or recliner is best, but you can use any comfortable chair or sofa. You can even use your bed, unless you tend to fall asleep when practicing.

➤ If the room is very cold and your muscles are tired, do not tense your muscles too tightly, or they may develop mild cramps.

➤ If you get a cramp, massage the muscle and stretch it out. The most common cramp is in the calf muscle. If this occurs, pulling the toes toward your face and massaging the calf muscle will usually relieve the cramp.

➤ Keeping the room at a comfortable temperature and being sure that your muscles are not tired should reduce the chance of cramping.

Each time you practice, be sure to fill out one Scanning Relaxation Rating Sheet before you practice and another one after you finish.

Give each student two copies of the Scanning Relaxation Rating Sheet to use for each day until your next session. Answer any questions.

Distress: The Alarm Reaction

AGENDA

1. Review of Session 1/Motivational Activity
2. Types of stress: Harmful stress (distress) and healthy stress (eustress)
3. Distress: Emergency reactions

   Nervous system messages

   Real Alarms and False Alarms

   Distress and illness
4. Scanning Relaxation
5. Home Practice: *Daily Scanning Relaxation*

MATERIALS

➤ Student Manuals

➤ Figures 3, 4, and 5 (reproduced in a whole-class format)

➤ A rubber snake and a pillowcase

➤ Scanning Relaxation CD and CD player

➤ Scanning Relaxation Rating Sheets (several copies for each student)

OBJECTIVES

Students will . . .

1. Review the main concepts presented in Session 1: labeling stress, behavioral and physiological signs of stress, muscle tensing and relaxing, Scanning Relaxation.
2. Understand the difference between harmful and healthy stress.
3. Be able to distinguish between Real Alarms and False Alarms, both of which result in "emergency reactions" to stressors.
4. Recognize the connection between continued distress and physical illness.
5. Continue to practice Scanning Relaxation.

PROCEDURE

Review of Session 1/Motivational Activity

Before students arrive, put the rubber snake in the pillowcase. When they have been seated, tell them that you will be pulling a snake out of the pillowcase but that the snake is not real. Then take out the snake, and have the group discuss how they would feel if the snake were real.

During the last session we talked about **SIGNS OF STRESS**— the different ways our bodies show that we're upset or tense.

Ask the group for examples.

We've also talked about **STRESSORS,** or things that trigger stress reactions. Stressors can be *outside* us or *inside* us.

Ask the group for examples of each type. Sample answers for external stressors include being cold, being chased by a tiger, or having an argument with a parent. Internal stressors might include worried thoughts or images about giving a presentation in front of the class, going to the dentist, or taking the test for your driver's license.

Turn to **page 11** in your Student Manuals. Let's look at what happens to the people in the stories on this page and the next, and try to identify the signs of stress and the stressors involved in each.

Ask for a volunteer to read the first story. Have the group write down the answers to the questions in their manuals, then ask for volunteers to give the answers aloud. Do the same for the four remaining stories. For the fifth story, ask the following question.

How is the stressor different in the story about Mary, who goes to bed but suddenly remembers she has a book report due?

Elicit the idea that it isn't an external stressor that causes Mary's stress, but an internal stressor—her worried thoughts about not being able to finish the book report.

Share an experience of stress you have had since the last session, then ask students to do the same.

Types of Stress

*Refer students to the whole-class display of Figure 3, which also appears on **page 13** in their manuals. Discuss the following.*

➤ We learned that the **STRESSOR** is the force that starts everything, the trigger. *(Point to the word* stressor *on the figure.)*

➤ **STRESS** is a person's reaction to the stressor.

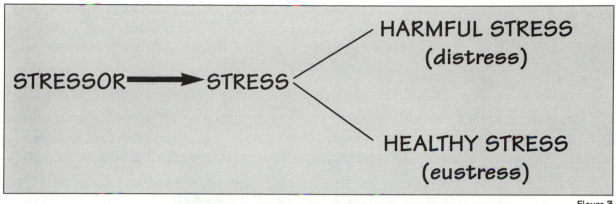

STRESSOR � STRESS < HARMFUL STRESS (distress) / HEALTHY STRESS (eustress)

Figure 3

➤ Stress isn't nervous tension. It can be either harmful and unpleasant, what we call **DISTRESS** *(point),* or it can be healthy and pleasant, called **EUSTRESS** *(point).*

➤ Harmful stress, or **DISTRESS,** includes all the negative reactions to upsetting situations we've talked about so far. Distress is *unpleasant* stress, like a pounding heart, sweating hands, and an upset stomach when you're alone at home at night after watching a horror movie and hear strange noises outside your bedroom door.

➤ **EUSTRESS,** or healthy stress, refers to the stress you feel from doing *pleasant* things, such as dancing, exercising, going on a vacation, and so forth.

So it's not just bad things that happen to us that can cause us stress—it's also good things.

At the beginning of the session, we talked about different people's signs of stress and their stressors. In Theresa's story, Theresa feels stress when a guy she likes sits down next to her in study hall.

What other positive events might cause stress—that is, healthy stress or eustress?

Discuss. Students might mention situations like getting to play in a big game, moving to a new neighborhood, or going away to college.

The only time you are stress-free is when you are dead. Otherwise, you are reacting either positively or negatively to the people and things around you and to the situations in which you find yourself.

Distress: Emergency Reactions

Let's look together at a specific example of a situation (a stressor) that causes **DISTRESS:**

You're crossing the street, thinking about something and not really paying much attention. All of a sudden, you hear a loud horn and see a big bus bearing down on you. How do you react?

Elicit answers from students. Responses might include jumping away, yelling for help, and the like.

In this situation, the bus is the stressor, and you react with distress. Your body has what we call an **EMERGENCY REACTION.**

Look at the picture of the cat on **page 13** in your manuals. This cat is having an **EMERGENCY REACTION.**

Give students a chance to look at the picture, then ask the following questions.

➤ How do you think this cat feels?

➤ Have you ever felt this way? *(Encourage students to describe the situations and their feelings.)*

➤ How do your muscles feel when you are having an emergency reaction?

➤ How is that different from the way your muscles feel after you practice your Scanning Relaxation exercise?

Nervous System Messages

Your brain sends messages to other parts of your body through the **NERVOUS SYSTEM.**

Turn to **page 14** in your manuals. This is a picture of the **NERVOUS SYSTEM,** showing all the nerve paths to and from the brain. Notice that there are *many* nerve paths for sending messages to and from the brain.

When you have an emergency reaction, your brain sends messages through the nervous system to various parts of the body, then those parts react with stress. If you look at the diagram on **page 15,** you can see how this works.

Show the whole-class version of Figure 4 and discuss.

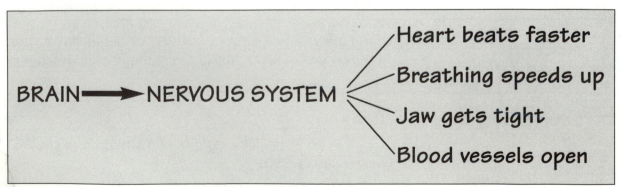

BRAIN ⟶ NERVOUS SYSTEM
- Heart beats faster
- Breathing speeds up
- Jaw gets tight
- Blood vessels open

Figure 4

If the stressor is not very threatening, only certain parts of your body react and not others. For example, your heart may beat very fast, but your palms may not get sweaty (or the other way around).

When the danger (the stressor) is gone, your brain (through the nervous system) tells various parts of your body to relax, slow down, and go back to their normal state. For example, your heartbeat and breathing slow down. Everything goes back to normal.

Real Alarms and False Alarms

Look again at **page 15** in your manuals. The emergency reaction to a real threat is very important if we are going to survive danger. A real threat might be finding yourself on the ledge of a ten-story building or having an armed robber point a gun at you.

In both cases, a real threat sets off a **REAL ALARM** in your brain, which triggers an emergency reaction in your body. Your heart beats faster, you feel short of breath, your stomach churns, and so on.

Ask students to generate and write some other examples of Real Alarms.

But sometimes you might have an emergency reaction to a **FALSE ALARM.** That means you have an emergency reaction (either a full-scale or "mini" reaction) to all kinds of stressors that you *think* might become threats. For example:

> ➤ You look out the window of a ten-story building and think that the window might open or give way and you'll be pulled out through it. You get so upset, you fall to your knees.

> ➤ You see a man in line at the bus stop with a small brown bag, and you think, "I wonder if he has a gun in the bag and plans to rob the bus!" You break out in a sweat.

The window, of course, does not move, and the man pulls out a hero sandwich, not a gun, but both times the False Alarm caused your body to go through an emergency reaction. Your muscles tightened, your stomach churned, your heart beat faster, and so forth.

Have students come up with and write down other examples of False Alarms.

Even though you only imagine a threat, your body reacts as if it is real.

You can have an emergency reaction to a wide range of stressors—worries about school, arguments with your parents or your friends, being threatened by another student, and other less extreme situations.

Distress and Illness

There is a problem if you have **REAL ALARMS** or **FALSE ALARMS** all the time: You can become exhausted and ill. Distress over a long period of time reduces your resistance to disease.

*Direct students to **page 16** in their manuals, and show the whole-class version of Figure 5. Have each student fill in a personal stressor (source of worry), then briefly discuss.*

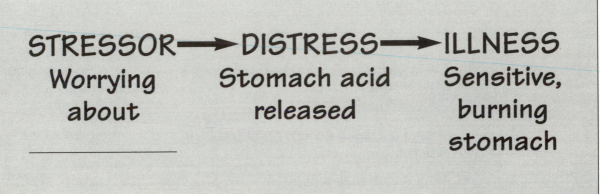

STRESSOR ➞ DISTRESS ➞ ILLNESS
Worrying about _____   Stomach acid released   Sensitive, burning stomach

Figure 5

Even if your stomach isn't burning, the acid your stomach releases can wear away the stomach lining, making your stomach sensitive when you eat spicy foods like pepperoni pizza. You may even vomit.

If this goes on for a long time, you can even develop an ulcer. This means the acid actually burns a hole in your stomach lining.

All the body's signs of stress are important. **Listen to what your body is telling you!** It may be telling you that it is getting worn down by too many Real and False Alarms.

Give students an opportunity to discuss.

Scanning Relaxation

Discuss students' experiences during home practice with the Scanning Relaxation CD.

1. Use the Scanning Relaxation Rating Sheets students filled out as a basis for discussion. Point out that the rating sheet

is intended for self-assessment, so it is important to be honest when filling it out.

2. Troubleshoot problems during practice.

3. Discuss parts of the body that were the most difficult to relax.

Conduct Scanning Relaxation practice according to the procedures described in Session 1. Collect students' filled-out Scanning Relaxation Rating Sheets.

Home Practice

*Ask students to practice Scanning Relaxation at least once daily and to fill out a Scanning Relaxation Rating Sheet before and after each practice. Briefly go over the guidelines at the bottom of **page 16** of the Student Manual.*

Distribute enough rating sheets so each student has two per day until the next session.

The Mind-Body Connection

AGENDA

1. Scanning Relaxation
2. Review of Session 2/Motivational Activity
3. Comfort zones
4. Stress filters
5. Home Practice: *Daily Scanning Relaxation*

MATERIALS

➤ Student Manuals
➤ Figures 6, 7, and 8 (reproduced in a whole-class format)
➤ Scanning Relaxation CD and CD player
➤ Scanning Relaxation Rating Sheets (several copies for each student)

OBJECTIVES

Students will . . .

1. Review the main concepts presented in Session 2: distress and eustress, emergency reactions, Real Alarms and False Alarms.
2. Understand the concept of comfort zones with regard to stress and be able to determine their own comfort zones.
3. Recognize the advantages of having broad comfort zones with regard to stress.
4. Comprehend the idea that people have stress filters that vary in their effectiveness in screening out stress.
5. Become aware that stress enters the body through the mind—that is, that the mind functions as the stress filter.

PROCEDURE

Scanning Relaxation

Begin by conducting Scanning Relaxation with the CD, following the procedures in Session 1. Have the students fill out a Scanning Relaxation Rating Sheet before and after practice. Address any comments or questions about home practice, then collect the Scanning Relaxation Rating Sheets.

Review of Session 2/Motivational Activity

*Refer students to the story on **page 17** in their Student Manuals. Read or have a student read the story aloud, then ask the discussion questions.*

Remembering what we talked about during the last session, let's see if we can understand what was happening to Luci.

1. What happened to Luci each time the phone rang?

Luci experienced physiological reactions of distress (in the order Luci experienced them): jumpiness, heart pounding, shortness of breath; bloated, upset stomach; tiredness; headache; tightness and stiffness of jaw and neck muscles; shaky hands, queasy stomach. Label these responses emergency reactions to False Alarms.

2. Why was Luci headachy and tired by the end of the day?

Luci felt this way because frequent False Alarms kept her body in a state of emergency reaction (for example, her muscles were tensed and tight all day).

3. Who or what were the stressors in this story?

Stressors were Luci's own thoughts, the phone ringing, and Mr. Wilson.

4. What do we call the harmful reactions Luci was experiencing?

Answer: Distress.

Comfort Zones

During the last session we talked about how people experience and show distress in different ways. Some people get headaches. Others get gassy, upset stomachs. Others feel very shaky and like crying.

People are also different in the amount of healthy stress or harmful distress they can deal with comfortably. People have different **COMFORT ZONES.**

Display the whole-class version of Figure 6.

COMFORT ZONE

Figure 6

Turn to **page 18** in your manuals. The pace of life and the number of unpleasant (and pleasant) activities people are comfortable with are different for each person. The amount of stress and distress a person feels comfortable dealing with is called the person's **COMFORT ZONE.**

To understand this idea more clearly, let's look at the comfort zones of six people: Jennie and Roberto, Keisha and Mike, and Lisa and Joe.

1. Jennie and Roberto are comfortable only in low gear, with a few exciting activities and very little distress. Long periods of noise and activity are stressors for them.

2. Keisha and Mike like to run at high gear all the time. They begin to get upset and feel distress if they're not doing something or going somewhere every minute.

Although these four are comfortable with their lifestyles, these lifestyles might not be healthy for them.

➤ Jennie and Roberto may not be able to deal with tough situations later in life and may spend much of their lives like the tortoise, hiding in their shells.

➤ Keisha and Mike may seem to be happy with their fast-paced life, but they may be able to keep up their pace only by keeping their bodies in Real Alarm or False Alarm all the time or by using stimulants like coffee or drugs.

3. Now let's look at Lisa and Joe. Their comfort zone is the widest. They can feel comfortable in fast-paced situations and in quieter, slower paced ones. They can handle a tough, demanding stressor and balance it with quiet, relaxing time to give their bodies and minds a chance to refresh themselves.

We all need to learn about our own comfort zones so we can live at a pace that keeps our distress at low levels. We are also learning techniques that may help us broaden our comfort zones to deal with more of the situations we will face in our lives.

Where is your **COMFORT ZONE** on the diagram?

Have students mark the diagram to show their present comfort zones, then discuss. Emphasize the need to develop a wide comfort zone and to balance times when they are in high and low gear.

Stress Filters

One reason we have different comfort zones is that we each also have a different **STRESS FILTER.**

Display Figure 7 in a whole-class format.

STRESS FILTER

Figure 7

What do you think I mean by a **STRESS FILTER?**

What is a filter—what does it do—for example, on a water faucet? *(It keeps dirt or harmful substances from getting into the water we use.)*

A stress filter determines how much stress gets into our bodies and makes us react. What, really, then, is a stress filter?

Obviously, it isn't something we can see and touch like a water filter, and we don't have force fields around us as in *Star Wars* and other science fiction movies. The stress filter is your **MIND**—the way you see and think about the stressor.

Look at **page 19.** What we need to say to ourselves is: **Stress and distress enter my body through my mind.**

Display the whole-class version of Figure 8. Explain that this is the most important idea in the program and that you will be discussing it in more detail at the next session.

STRESS AND DISTRESS ENTER MY BODY THROUGH MY MIND

Figure 8

Home Practice

*Refer students to the instructions for home practice of Scanning Relaxation on **page 19** of their manuals. Ask students to practice Scanning Relaxation at least once daily and to fill out a Scanning Relaxation Rating Sheet before and after each practice.*

Distribute enough rating sheets so each student has two per day until the next session.

Self-Talk

AGENDA

1. Scanning Relaxation
2. Review of Session 3/Motivational Activity
3. Cognitive model of stress
   Automatic thoughts (self-talk)
   Meaning: danger or threat
   Self-talk and False Alarms
4. False Alarm Sheet
5. Home Practice:
   Practice Scanning Relaxation daily
   Use the False Alarm Sheet to record one False Alarm

MATERIALS

➤ Student Manuals
➤ Figure 8 (whole-class version; from Session 3); Figures 9 and 10 (reproduced in a whole-class format)
➤ Scanning Relaxation CD and CD player
➤ Scanning Relaxation Rating Sheets (several for each student)
➤ False Alarm Sheets (one per student)

OBJECTIVES

Students will . . .

1. Review the main concepts presented in Session 3: Comfort zones, stress filters, and the idea that stress enters the body through the mind.
2. Recognize that automatic thoughts determine whether or not something is a stressor for a person.
3. Understand that people experience distress whenever they feel something important to them is in danger (or there is a threat of danger).
4. Be able to distinguish between helpful self-talk and harmful self-talk (which causes False Alarms).

5. Begin to be able to analyze False Alarms through the use of the False Alarm Sheet.

PROCEDURE

Scanning Relaxation

Conduct Scanning Relaxation with the CD, following the procedures in Session 1. Have students fill out a Scanning Relaxation Rating Sheet before and after practice. Briefly discuss students' home practice, and collect the rating sheets.

Review of Session 3/Motivational Activity

How many of you have ever been in a group telling ghost stories or other scary stories—maybe at camp or at a Halloween party? How do you feel after everyone has been telling stories for a while?

Let students respond.

Let's say the stories are being told in a dark room that's very, very still and quiet. All of a sudden, someone behind you reaches over and places a hand on your shoulder. How would you react?

Encourage students to share their reactions.

What if someone did this to you during the day—let's say when you were walking down the hall to class? *(Students respond.)*

Why do you have such an extreme reaction during the storytelling and not on the way to class? Besides the hand on your shoulder, what stressor caused you to react so strongly?

Being touched during the day might make students feel mildly startled. What students were thinking about (the scary story) made their reactions much stronger.

Open your manuals to **page 21.** This page begins with a statement we learned during the last session.

> # STRESS AND DISTRESS ENTER MY BODY THROUGH MY MIND

Figure 8

➤ You feel distress because you **THINK** something is a threat.
➤ Because you **THINK** it is a threat, it is a stressor for you.

Cognitive Model of Stress

*Continue with **page 21** in the Student Manual.*

We all share some of the same stressors. For example, being in a building that is on fire or being in the path of a raging bull are stressors for all of us. Can you think of other stressors we might have in common?

Encourage responses, and ask students to record a few in the blanks. Sample answers include being in an earthquake or locking yourself out of your house or car.

Even though we have many stressors in common, the things that are stressors for one person are not necessarily stressors for another person. For example, suppose two teenage girls enter a friend's house, and a large dog comes up to greet them.

*Have students turn to **page 22**.*

➤ One girl—let's call her Julia—feels a hot rush through her body, feels her heart begin to race, screams, and runs out the door. For Julia, the dog is a stressor, and she has an emergency reaction from this False Alarm. The stressor—the dog—leads to **DISTRESS** for Julia.

➤ The other girl—let's call her Cindy—sees the dog and has warm, happy feelings. She quickly moves toward the dog and pets him while he licks her face. For Cindy, the sight of the dog leads to healthy stress **(EUSTRESS).**

How can the same thing—the same dog—cause distress in one person and happy feelings in another?

*Let the group answer, then continue with the discussion on **page 22** in the Student Manual.*

Automatic Thoughts

How we react depends on what the thing or event means to us and what we say to ourselves about it.

When we see something—like a dog—very quick, short thoughts or pictures enter our minds almost automatically. These thoughts and pictures happen so fast that they are even called **AUTOMATIC THOUGHTS.** Sometimes we're not even aware that we have these thoughts or pictures in our minds.

Let's take Julia, for example. When she saw the dog, what do you think automatically came into her mind?

Take suggestions from the group.

These kind of thoughts are usually not a whole sentence, but words like "dog–bite–run" or "dog–attack." Julia might also have brief pictures of the dog's teeth or the dog lunging toward her.

These thoughts or pictures are what set off the False Alarm and cause the emergency reaction.

Now let's look at Cindy. What do you think came automatically into Cindy's mind?

Encourage responses.

Cindy sees the dog, and words like "cute" and "friendly" come to her mind. She pictures the dog licking her, so she reacts with warm, happy feelings.

*Have students share thoughts and images that come to mind when they see or think about the things listed on **page 22** in their manuals.*

Meaning: Danger or Threat

Let's continue with **page 22** in your manuals. What the object or event **MEANS** to us is also important: What it means to us also determines whether it's a stressor or not. We feel distress whenever we believe that there is some danger or threat to anything that is important to us.

The key words are **DANGER** and **THREAT.**

*Refer students to **page 23** of the manual, and display the whole-class version of Figure 9.*

DANGER
THREAT

Figure 9

Julia believes the dog is a threat or danger to something important to her—what?

The threat is to her physical safety; she feels there is danger of pain and injury.

Let's say you have to make a speech in front of the whole class. As you go up before the class, you have a False Alarm and an emergency reaction: Your heart beats faster, the palms of your hands perspire, and your body shakes.

Why? What important thing do you feel or think is threatened or in danger?

Discuss, then have students record their answers. Sample answers include the following.

➤ You may feel it threatens the way you want other people to think of you.

➤ You may be saying things to yourself like "People are going to think I'm stupid or boring—or both."

➤ You think you're going to start shaking or faint in front of the group.

Because what people think about you is important to you, this threat causes you to feel distress. How do you feel this distress?

Encourage students to identify their own physiological signs.

If you didn't care what anyone thought, what would you say to yourself?

Encourage students to discuss and record their answers. Sample answers include the following.

➤ Who cares what people think? I know I'm smart and interesting.

➤ I'm going to be terrific!

➤ Hey, I can handle this.

If you say these kinds of things, you don't feel any distress. Instead you might feel excited about getting up in front of the class (eustress).

Self-Talk and False Alarms

*Continue with **page 23** in the Student Manual. Display Figure 10 in a whole-class format.*

SELF-TALK

Figure 10

What we tell ourselves about a situation is called **SELF-TALK.**

Sometimes what we say to ourselves—our automatic thoughts or **SELF-TALK**—about danger is a very good thing. For example, if the dog is a Doberman trained to kill and about to lunge at Julia, Julia's telling herself that the dog is dangerous and running away is the best way to react to the situation because it is a **REAL ALARM**.

But it's not healthy to have a **FALSE ALARM** and an emergency reaction at the sight of every dog: These fears are bad for our bodies and keep us from doing lots of things we'd like to do— for example, visiting friends who have dogs.

What are some other things that might cause you to have a False Alarm and an emergency reaction?

Sample answers include seeing a bug, riding in an elevator, looking out a tenth-story window, going to a job interview, and meeting new people.

False Alarm Sheet

Sometimes we have to watch ourselves really closely to figure out what we are saying to ourselves or picturing in our minds and what the thing or situation means to us.

Between now and the next session, find one time when you had a False Alarm (something that really wasn't an emergency situation) and you responded to it with an emergency reaction. We'll use the False Alarm Sheet.

Let's fill out the example on **page 24** in your manuals to make sure everyone knows what to do.

Use the following to illustrate use of the False Alarm Sheet.

1. Stressor (What happened?): *I lost my hairbrush.*
2. Self-talk: *I look a mess. Everyone is going to think I look ugly.*
3. Meaning (Why was this important to me?): *I think people will say I'm too lazy and sloppy to brush my hair.*
4. Physiological (body) reactions: *Felt jumpy all day long, stomach upset, neck muscles tight.*

Ask if there are any questions; clarify the assignment as needed.

Remember, this was a False Alarm because you were not in any real, life-threatening danger. We'll look at your False Alarm Sheets together next week. Don't make your example too personal, so you can share it with the group.

Home Practice

*Refer students to **page 25** in the Student Manual.*

1. Ask students to practice Scanning Relaxation at least once daily and to fill out a Scanning Relaxation Rating Sheet before and after each practice.

Distribute rating sheets as needed.

2. Give each student a copy of the False Alarm Sheet. Instruct students to fill the sheet out before the next session.

Calm Body, Clear Mind

AGENDA

1. Scanning Relaxation
2. Review of Session 4/Motivational Activity
3. Reducing emergency reactions
4. Introduction to Calm Body, Clear Mind
   Calm Body: Quick Body Scanning
   Clear Mind: Correct self-talk
   Calm Body, Clear Mind examples
5. Home Practice
   Daily Scanning Relaxation practice
   Quick Body Scanning three times per day (more if needed)

MATERIALS

➤ Student Manuals
➤ Figures 11 and 12 (reproduced in a whole-class format)
➤ Scanning Relaxation CD and CD player
➤ Scanning Relaxation Rating Sheets
➤ Steps in Quick Body Scanning handout (from Appendix B)

OBJECTIVES

Students will . . .

1. Review the main concepts presented in Session 4: the cognitive model of stress (automatic thoughts, danger and threat, self-talk and False Alarms).
2. Be able to employ the Calm Body technique via the Quick Body Scanning procedure.
3. Begin to understand the components of the Clear Mind technique through examples provided of correct facts and correct meaning.
4. Recognize the words *Calm Body, Clear Mind* as cues to use these techniques to deal with Real Alarms and False Alarms.

PROCEDURE

Scanning Relaxation

Let's start with the Scanning Relaxation together. Remember to inhale *slowly*, then exhale and say to yourself, "Relax and let go." Breathe gently and normally.

Conduct Scanning Relaxation with the CD, following the procedures in Session 1. Have students fill out a Scanning Relaxation Rating Sheet before and after practice. Collect these and any sheets from home practice. Briefly address any questions or comments about the home practice.

Review of Session 4/Motivational Activity

Let's look at two different situations and try to figure out what the person is thinking in each. Turn to **page 27** in your manuals.

Read or have a volunteer read Tommy's situation aloud, then have the group answer the following questions.

➤ What was Tommy saying to himself? *(Sample answer: "That poisonous beetle is going to jump on me and bite me.")*

➤ What important thing did Tommy feel was in danger? *(his life, his personal safety)*

Read or have a volunteer read the situation involving Min aloud, then have the group answer the following questions.

➤ What was Min thinking? *(Sample answer: "They think I look weird and ugly.")*

➤ What important thing did Min feel was in danger? *(her sense of worth as a person)*

In the last session, you learned that stress and distress enter your body through what?

The answer is "Stress and distress enter my body through my mind."

What we say to ourselves about a situation—our **SELF-TALK**—determines whether or not we react with distress.

For example, saying to myself, "That's a snake, and it is going to bite me and poison me" will signal a False Alarm and an emergency reaction. If I say to myself instead, "That is a piece of rope," I don't have the emergency reaction, and there is no distress.

Let's go over the False Alarm Sheets you filled out since the last session.

Have volunteers give examples of False Alarms. Emphasize the points that self-talk causes reactions in the body and that these reactions depend upon the meaning the stressor has for us. Collect the sheets.

Reducing Emergency Reactions

For me to have an emergency reaction over a piece of rope, for Min to have an emergency reaction over some people looking at her, and for Tommy to have an emergency reaction over a beetle are all harmful overreactions.

Continue with **pages 27** *and* **28** *in the Student Manual.*

Emergency reactions need to be saved for real emergencies, Real Alarms. For good mental and physical health, we need to reduce as much of the unnecessary distress in our lives as possible.

We can't stop all the stressors in our lives—there are plenty of Real Alarms as well as False Alarms. But we *can* learn to handle stressors with as little pain and harm to us as possible. That is, we can try to reduce or lessen the stress a stressor makes us feel when, for example:

➤ Someone yells at us.

➤ We spill catsup on a new jacket.

➤ We lose our last turn on the video game.

➤ We miss the bus.

Can you name some other things that would be False Alarms?

Have students discuss and write down a few more False Alarms in their manuals.

Introduction to Calm Body, Clear Mind

Look at the middle of **page 28** in your manuals. You can reduce your alarm reactions, your emergency reactions, by doing two things:

➤ Calming your body down by using the relaxation techniques we've been learning.

➤ Changing what you say to yourself (your self-talk) to correct, accurate self-talk.

For example, Tommy could say to himself, "That is a harmless beetle," instead of "That monster is going to attack me!" Min could say to herself, "They probably look up at anyone new who enters the cafeteria."

A quick way for us to remember to do these two things when we feel a Real or False Alarm coming on, or anytime we're upset, is to say, **CALM BODY, CLEAR MIND.**

Display the whole-class version of Figure 11.

CALM BODY
CLEAR MIND

Figure 11

Calm Body: Quick Body Scanning

CALM BODY means we put our bodies into a state of relaxation—relax those tense muscles.

We've been practicing how to relax our muscles by using the Scanning Relaxation CD. But we can't practice the complete Scanning Relaxation exercise every time we meet a stressor or get upset.

So today we're going to learn a quicker technique that we can use anywhere, anytime to relax our muscles the way we do with the CD. This technique is called Quick Body Scanning.

Have students think of a stressor, then let their bodies relax as you read the instructions for Quick Body Scanning aloud. The script for Quick Body Scanning appears in Appendix A.

When you have finished, give each student a copy of the Steps in Quick Body Scanning handout. Explain that students can carry the handout with them; show them how they can fold the sheet and put it in a pocket.

Clear Mind: Correct Self-Talk

Look at **page 29** in your manuals. **CLEAR MIND** means thinking clearly and correctly. This means that our self-talk is correct in **FACTS** and correct in **MEANING.**

Display the whole-class version of Figure 12.

CLEAR MIND = SELF-TALK WITH   1. Correct facts
2. Correct meaning

Figure 12

If we think back to Tommy's situation, does Tommy have correct facts about the beetle?

➤ Tommy thinks: "That poisonous beetle is going to jump on me and bite me." *(incorrect fact)*

➤ Tommy thinks: "That's just a harmless beetle—it won't hurt me." *(correct fact)*

What about Min? Does Min have the correct facts and correct meaning when she thinks about the people looking at her in the cafeteria of her new school?

➤ Min thinks: "People are looking at me." *(correct fact)*

➤ Min thinks: "They think I look weird and ugly." *(incorrect meaning)*

Does Min know for sure that the people in the cafeteria are looking at her because they think she looks weird and ugly? Is there anything else their looking at her could mean? What could Min think instead?

Min might think, "If people look at me, it doesn't mean there is anything wrong with me" or "They probably look at anyone new who walks in."

Calm Body, Clear Mind Examples

Let's practice applying the Calm Body, Clear Mind techniques in another situation. Look at Situation 1 on **page 29** in your manuals. Here's how this might work.

➤ Situation: You and your friend disagree over whether the new CD you just bought is any good or not.

➤ Calm Body: As you feel yourself getting upset, you think, "Calm Body," and relax your muscles from the head down, using Quick Body Scanning.

➤ Clear Mind: Say to yourself, "Clear Mind." This reminds you to check—

Correct facts: My friend said she didn't like my new CD, not that she didn't like me.

Correct meaning: We can still be friends and like each other without agreeing on everything. If my friend disagrees with me, that doesn't mean he or she has stopped liking me.

Ask students to think of real-life situations in which they could apply the Calm Body, Clear Mind techniques. Choose and process a student example as Situation 2, then discuss.

Let's quickly review what we've talked about today. We have learned some **CUES** to help us deal with Real and False Alarms.

Cues are reminders, short phrases we say to ourselves. What are the cues we learned today? *(Calm Body, Clear Mind)*

We emphasized that when we cue ourselves with Clear Mind, it's important to make sure that not only the *facts* but also the *meaning* of these facts are correct and not exaggerated.

Home Practice

*Refer students to the middle of **page 30** in their manuals.*

1. Continue using the CD to practice Scanning Relaxation at least once a day until the next session. Fill out a Scanning Relaxation Rating Sheet *before* and *after* each practice.

Distribute Scanning Relaxation Rating Sheets as needed.

2. Practice Quick Body Scanning during the day. Use your Steps in Quick Body Scanning handout until you know how to do the scan without the sheet. Do the scan as often as you need it, but at least three times a day.

Meaning

AGENDA

1. Scanning Relaxation
2. Review of Session 5/Motivational Activity
3. Identifying correct meaning
4. Calm Body, Clear Mind exercises
5. Calm Body, Clear Mind Cue Sheets
6. Home Practice

   Scanning Relaxation with rating sheet at least twice a week until the next session

   Quick Body Scanning as needed in various settings

   Calm Body, Clear Mind techniques with cue sheet at least once daily

MATERIALS

➤ Student Manuals
➤ Scanning Relaxation CD and CD player
➤ Scanning Relaxation Rating Sheets
➤ Calm Body, Clear Mind Cue Sheets

OBJECTIVES

Students will . . .

1. Review the main concepts presented in Session 5: reducing emergency reactions by using Calm Body (Quick Body Scanning) and Clear Mind (correct facts and correct meaning).
2. Identify what they believe is personally important and would result in distress if it were endangered.
3. Recognize when their self-talk about a situation includes incorrect or exaggerated meanings.
4. Complete Calm Body, Clear Mind exercises, with the group and individually.

   Select a stressor that triggers a False Alarm.

   Recognize the physiological reactions to the False Alarm.

   Identify self-talk in reference to individual triggers/stressors.

   Employ the Calm Body, Clear Mind techniques.

5. Learn the purpose of the Calm Body, Clear Mind Cue Sheet.

PROCEDURE

Scanning Relaxation

Conduct Scanning Relaxation with the CD, following the procedures in Session 1. Have students fill out a Scanning Relaxation Rating Sheet before and after practice. Collect these and any rating sheets from home practice, and address any questions or comments. Discuss students' use of the Quick Body Scanning technique; review the procedure if necessary.

Review of Session 5/Motivational Activity

Turn to **page 31** in your manuals. Write your name on the line in the box.

Now fill this page with words that describe all the things that are important to you: people, places, beliefs, your own talents and characteristics—anything.

Give the group a few minutes to write their responses.

Now circle the five or six things that are most important to you.

When you think there is any danger of something bad happening to any of the things you circled, what do you feel?

Sample answers: Upset, anxious, worried. (Sum up the answers with the word distress.*)*

We feel distress only when we think there is a danger that something important to us will be lost or harmed.

➤ If it's not important, then we don't react with distress.

➤ When you have a Real Alarm or a False Alarm, there's a good chance your reaction has something to do with one of the things you wrote down—or it's something you should add to your page.

But we have also learned that people, places, and things don't directly cause us to feel distress. How do stress and distress enter your body?

Answer: "Stress and distress enter my body through my mind."

Identifying Correct Meaning

Let's say you wrote down your best friend's name on the page in your manual:

Today, when your friend passes you in the hall, he or she barely even notices you instead of stopping to talk as usual. During the day, brief pictures of your friend walking away down the hall keep flashing in your mind. When they do, you tighten your jaw and stomach muscles. By lunchtime you're feeling a little shaky and headachy. Now your friend comes up to you and says, "Hey, let's have lunch. I was really worried about a test I had to take this morning, but now that it's over, I feel great." You breathe out a long sigh and say, "I thought you were mad at me or something this morning!"

You could have saved yourself a whole morning of distress from this False Alarm by remembering the two cues we learned last week. When we feel a Real Alarm or a False Alarm, what do we say to ourselves?

Answer: Calm Body, Clear Mind.

What do these words mean?

➤ *Calm Body* means putting your body into a state of relaxation—relaxing your tense muscles through body scanning.

➤ *Clear Mind* means changing what you say to yourself so your self-talk is correct (this means correct facts and correct meaning).

In the situation we just discussed, what were you probably saying to yourself about this False Alarm that was causing your emergency reaction?

Sample answer: My friend is really mad at me and doesn't want to be around me anymore.

What did your friend's behavior mean to you? What did you feel you were in danger of losing?

Sample answers: The person's friendship, your best friend.

What does *Clear Mind* mean in this situation?

➤ *Correct facts:* Your friend was in a rush this morning and did not stop to speak with you.

➤ *Correct meaning:* Something must be bothering your friend.

Turn to **page 32** in your manuals. Sometimes our **FACTS** are correct, but the **MEANING** we give them is wrong or exaggerated, blown up out of proportion.

For example, let's say that your friend really *is* mad at you about something—that happens sometimes between friends. You would be right to say to yourself, "My friend is mad at me." This is a correct fact. But that alone wouldn't send you into an emergency reaction.

What you think your friend's being mad at you **MEANS** is what makes you upset. It's because you say things like this to yourself:

> ➤ He or she doesn't want to be friends anymore.

> ➤ If I lose this friendship, I'll never have a friend again.

> ➤ If my friend doesn't like me anymore, it must be because there's something really wrong with me.

The **FACT** is correct: Your friend *is* mad at you. But your self-talk about the **MEANING** is incorrect: It didn't mean *any* of those things you said to yourself.

So let's look at the right way to deal with this situation: We feel ourselves getting upset, so we say to ourselves, **CALM BODY, CLEAR MIND.**

> ➤ *Calm Body:* We scan our bodies for muscle tension and relax and let the tension go. (We do our Quick Body Scanning.)

> ➤ *Clear Mind:* We have correct facts ("Yes, my friend is mad at me") and correct meaning. What would the correct meaning be?

Encourage students to write an answer in the blank. Sample responses: It bothers me when we fight, but we've always worked it out before; it's normal for friends to fight sometimes.

Many times when we're upset, it's the false or incorrect **MEANING** we give the situation that makes us feel so bad.

*Discuss and help students correct the meanings in the examples on **page 32** of their manuals.*

1. If he or she doesn't go out with me, it means I'm a loser. *(Correct meaning: He or she is the one who loses by missing a chance to be with me.)*

2. If I don't get an A or B on this test, it means I'm stupid. *(Correct meaning: It means I need to change the way I study, how much I study, or get help to catch up with information or skills I haven't learned.)*

The hardest part of using the Clear Mind technique is making sure we have the correct meaning. It's really easy for all of us to overreact and feel as though something that happens is the end of the world for us. Usually, though, most things aren't as terrible as we make them seem at first.

One way to keep from overreacting is to try to think of other possible meanings, in the way we just did for these two examples. Remember, we're talking about False Alarms, not Real Alarms, here. We don't want to pretend that real threats and dangers don't exist.

We want to save our emergency reactions for these real threats rather than react to everyday events that are not Real Alarms with distress (an upset stomach, a headache, shakiness, and so on).

Even in a real emergency, the Calm Body, Clear Mind techniques can help us stay in enough control to decide how best to handle the situation.

Remember that the words **CALM BODY, CLEAR MIND** are **CUES** to help you remember what to do.

➤ *Calm Body* means to scan your body for muscle tension, then relax and let go.

➤ *Clear Mind* means you get the correct facts and correct meaning.

Calm Body, Clear Mind Exercises

When we're really upset, it's often hard to remember what we need to do to calm ourselves down. What helps is practicing the techniques when we're not so upset.

We're going to practice using the Calm Body, Clear Mind techniques so they will become a habit that we can begin to use automatically to deal with Real and False Alarms.

Have students suggest an example of something that has happened or could happen to trigger a False Alarm. Together, complete Calm Body, Clear Mind Exercise 1, on **page 33** *in their manuals.*

Next have each student complete Calm Body, Clear Mind Exercise 2 **(page 34)** *individually, followed by sharing and discussion.*

Calm Body, Clear Mind Cue Sheets

Have students turn to **page 35** *in their manuals. Explain that Calm Body, Clear Mind Cue Sheets are a way to keep track of how well these techniques are working for them.*

Have students put their names and the date at the top, then write a word or two to describe the situation and circle how they felt after using the techniques in Calm Body, Clear Mind Exercise 2.

Home Practice

Continue with **page 35** *in the Student Manual.*

1. Continue using the CD to practice Scanning Relaxation at least twice a week until the next meeting (more if desired). Fill out a Scanning Relaxation Rating Sheet *before* and *after* each practice.

Give each student as many Scanning Relaxation Rating Sheets as necessary.

2. Continue using Quick Body Scanning in various settings as needed.

3. Practice the Calm Body, Clear Mind techniques at least once a day.

   ➤ *Calm Body:* Quick Body Scanning.

   ➤ *Clear Mind:* Self-talk with correct facts and correct meaning.

   Complete a Calm Body, Clear Mind Cue Sheet each time you practice.

   ➤ Write your name and the date at the top.

   ➤ Write a word or two to describe what was happening to you before you used Calm Body, Clear Mind. Circle whether using these techniques made you feel much better, better, slightly better, the same, or worse.

   ➤ Use a different sheet each day.

Give each student one cue sheet for each day until the next session. Show students how to fold each page into quarters so they expose a different cue sheet each day.

Calming Actions

AGENDA

1. Quick Body Scanning
2. Review of Session 6/Motivational Activity
3. Behavioral and affective coping: Calming Actions

   Let feelings out

   Talk about feelings

   Exercise

   Rest

   Use distraction
4. Calming Actions Cue Sheets
5. Home Practice

   Scanning Relaxation with rating sheet at least twice before the next session

   Quick Body Scanning and Calm Body, Clear Mind techniques as needed in various settings

   Daily practice of a Calming Action technique with cue sheet

MATERIALS

➤ Student Manuals

➤ Figures 13–19 (reproduced in a whole-class format)

➤ Scanning Relaxation Rating Sheets

➤ Calming Actions Cue Sheets

OBJECTIVES

Students will . . .

1. Review the main concepts presented in Session 6: Applying the Calm Body, Clear Mind techniques to specific situations.
2. Recognize the benefits of five specific behavioral and affective coping techniques in dealing with stress.
2. Be able to provide specific examples of their own use of these coping techniques.
3. Recognize the words *Calming Actions* as a cue to engage in these coping techniques.

PROCEDURE

Quick Body Scanning

Have students practice Quick Body Scanning (read the complete script in Appendix A). Address any comments or questions about Scanning Relaxation home practice, then collect the Scanning Relaxation Rating Sheets. Answer any questions about students' use of Quick Body Scanning.

Review of Session 6/Motivational Activity

In the last session, we talked about using the Calm Body, Clear Mind techniques. Turn to **page 37** in your manuals. Take a moment to write down one of the situations you practiced, then describe how these techniques worked for you.

Give students a minute or two to write, then have volunteers give examples of their use of the Calm Body, Clear Mind techniques. Reinforce participation and troubleshoot as needed, then collect the students' Calm Body, Clear Mind Cue Sheets, completed as home practice.

Behavioral and Affective Coping: Calming Actions

Let's continue with **page 37** in the Student Manual. So far, we've learned how to handle situations that upset us—cause us to feel distress—by changing the way we *react* in our bodies and our minds.

Now we're going to learn some more *active* ways of dealing with stressors. We can use these methods once we've gotten ourselves under control by using the Calm Body, Clear Mind techniques.

Once we have ourselves calmed down and thinking clearly, it's time to take action. We can do one of two things. Turn to **page 38** in your manuals.

Display the whole-class version of Figure 13.

1. Work out more feelings of tension and distress
2. Try to solve the problem

Figure 13

In this session, we'll talk about the first idea, the various things we can do to work out more of the tension and distress.

Display the whole-class version of Figure 14.

LET FEELINGS OUT

Figure 14

The first way is to **LET FEELINGS OUT.** To do this, people sometimes cry and sometimes yell. Write the words *crying* and *yelling* in your manuals on the first two lines.

Let's pretend right now that you feel like crying but are trying not to. Tell me what you do to hold back the tears.

A common response is to tighten muscles, especially in the jaw.

Sometimes relaxing your muscles through Calm Body and changing your self-talk through Clear Mind will be enough to take away the feeling that you need to cry.

At other times, the need to cry is so strong that it doesn't let you relax those muscles. That's when it helps to cry out that muscle tension and all those bottled-up feelings.

You probably don't want to be crying to release tension all or most of the time, but when you need to, crying is a good, healthy way to let out tension and distress.

Once you've let out all that tightness through crying, then you'll be able to use your Calm Body, Clear Mind techniques to keep the tension and distress from building up again.

Can you think of times when it would be a good release of stress to let yourself cry?

Have volunteers give answers. Sample responses include when someone they care for (a person or even an animal) passes away or when they see something terrible happen to others.

Some people don't feel like crying when they feel distress. Instead, they feel like yelling or making other sounds. *(Demonstrate some guttural sounds.)*

It's almost as though the sounds are building up inside until they feel like a big balloon that might pop. Have any of you ever felt that way?

Encourage the group to share.

If we wait too long, we can lose control of these feelings and yell at people for no reason at all or make a big yelling scene over something not very important. We "blow up."

Ask the group to share experiences briefly.

It's better if we let a little of these feelings out at a time so we don't blow up and make everyone around us stressed out. We can do this in a number of ways:

➤ We can go to our rooms or sit in the car by ourselves to let out some of these sounds for a short time.

➤ We can put on some loud music and belt out our feelings with it. We can also clench our fists and shake our arms or stomp our feet to the music.

➤ We can even yell in our imaginations: We can close our eyes and picture ourselves standing alone on a big hill, on the edge of the Grand Canyon or any other big, empty place, yelling at the top of our lungs until we feel all yelled out.

Let's practice yelling together, in our imaginations:

> Close your eyes. Now picture yourself in this wide, open space alone. See yourself lift your arms, lift your face, and feel yourself yell. Yell, yell, yell louder. Keep yelling into the open space. Feel the sounds coming out of your throat. Yell, yell, yell louder. When you've finished yelling, rest your arms and do your Quick Body Scanning.

Conduct Quick Body Scanning by reading the following steps in Quick Body Scanning (do not read the numbers).

Steps in Quick Body Scanning

1. As you breathe in, scan your face, neck, shoulders, and arms.
2. As you breathe out, feel any tension slip away.
3. As you breathe in, scan your chest, lungs, and stomach.
4. As you breathe out, feel any tension slip away.
5. As you breathe in, scan your hips, legs, and feet.
6. As you breathe out, feel any tension slip away.

Now add *imaginary yelling* as number 3 on **page 38** in your manuals.

How else can you let out feelings besides crying or yelling? Use the two remaining lines to write down some of your own ideas.

Encourage students to share their ideas. Give taking a bath or a shower as a suggestion. Have students add these ideas to their lists.

Next display the whole-class version of Figure 15.

TALK ABOUT FEELINGS

Figure 15

The Calm Body, Clear Mind techniques help take care of Real Alarms and False Alarms at the times they happen. But if we **TALK ABOUT FEELINGS** with someone who cares and will listen, it helps us work out more of the tension and distress and may even keep these feelings from coming back so easily.

Maybe that person is a friend, a teacher or counselor, your sister or brother, your aunt or uncle, or your parents. It's someone different for everyone, and maybe someone different depending upon whether the problem is schoolwork, your girlfriend or boyfriend, your parents, and so on.

Talking about feelings helps reduce the tension and distress we feel. Have you had any personal experiences of feeling less upset after talking to someone about your feelings?

Have volunteers share experiences.

On the blank lines at the bottom of **page 38,** write down the names of some people you could talk to about your feelings.

*Refer students to **page 39** in their manuals, then display the whole-class version of Figure 16.*

EXERCISE

Figure 16

Another way to reduce feelings of distress and tension is through **EXERCISE.** After we've used the Calm Body, Clear Mind techniques several times during the day, exercising our muscles is healthy for them.

Exercise can include everything from running and other aerobic activity to playing soccer, basketball, or any other sport to taking a walk around the block, dancing, or just slamming a tennis ball against a wall.

If you have a particular health problem or medical condition, you'll need to talk to your doctor about what exercise is right for you. For most people, even the simple exercise of walking is helpful.

What kind of exercise makes you feel better after you've been upset?

Have students write down their answers on the blank lines on **page 39,** *then ask volunteers to share.*

Sometimes a situation has been so upsetting that we feel very tired after it's over and we've calmed ourselves down with Calm Body, Clear Mind.

Display the whole-class version of Figure 17. Continue discussion.

REST

Figure 17

Then, to keep the distress and tension down, the best thing to do is to **REST** for a while. We handle situations best when we're rested. If we're tired, we tend to get upset and distressed more easily.

Can you recall a time when rest helped you handle an upsetting situation better?

Have each student write down a description of one situation in the space provided, then ask for volunteers to share. Refer students to **page 40** *in their manuals.*

So far, we've learned four actions in addition to Calm Body, Clear Mind that you might sometimes need to help reduce tension and distress. We'll call these **CALMING ACTIONS.**

Display the whole-class version of Figure 18.

CALMING ACTIONS
1. **Let feelings out**
2. **Talk about feelings**
3. **Exercise**
4. **Rest**

Figure 18

Sometimes it's not muscle tension that's the biggest problem, but those incorrect thoughts and images that keep popping into your mind. What are some of these incorrect thoughts and images?

Examples include images of needles and drills for tomorrow's dental appointment or worries about being ridiculed when giving an oral report to the class or being hit by a meteor.

You can use Calm Body, Clear Mind to deal with the distress and tension these thoughts and pictures cause you, but you'd probably like to find a way of just keeping these distressing thoughts out of your mind altogether.

Display the whole-class version of Figure 19.

USE DISTRACTION

Figure 19

In these cases, **DISTRACTION** helps. Using distraction means keeping ourselves and our minds too busy to let these thoughts and images, which we know are incorrect, constantly bother us.

Can you think of any distracting activities you could use? Write these in the spaces given on **page 40** in your manuals.

Invite students to share briefly. Answers include watching TV, listening to music, singing, playing games, going shopping, taking a drive, playing an instrument, doing housework, and playing with a pet.

Earlier, we learned two cues to help us cope with upsetting situations and the Real Alarms and False Alarms they can cause. What are they? *(Calm Body, Clear Mind)*

Today, we'll add a new cue: **CALMING ACTIONS.**

*Refer students to **page 41** in their manuals; display the whole-class version of Figure 20.*

CALMING ACTIONS

1. **Let feelings out**
2. **Talk about feelings**
3. **Exercise**
4. **Rest**
5. **Use distraction**

Figure 20

We don't need to use a Calming Action for every Real or False Alarm, but these actions can help us when we need to work out more tension or distress, or when we want to keep some of those distressing thoughts away.

Calming Actions Cue Sheets

Have students look at the sample Calming Actions Cue Sheet, on **page 41** *in their manuals. Explain that Calming Actions Cue Sheets are a way to keep track of how well the Calming Actions are working for them.*

Have students write their names and the date at the top, then give a word or two to describe a situation in which a Calming Action would be helpful. Then have students check off the Calming Action and how they think they would feel after using it.

Home Practice

Refer students to **page 42** *in their manuals, and give the following assignment.*

1. Continue using the CD to practice Scanning Relaxation at least twice a week until the next meeting (more if desired). Fill out a Scanning Relaxation Rating Sheet *before* and *after* each practice.

Distribute Scanning Relaxation Rating Sheets.

2. Continue using Quick Body Scanning and the Calm Body, Clear Mind techniques in various settings as needed.

Students should focus on cue sheets for Calming Actions; they do not need to fill out cue sheets for the Calm Body, Clear Mind techniques this time.

3. Practice a Calming Action at least once a day. Each time you practice, fill out a Calming Actions Cue Sheet.

➤ Write your name and the date at the top.

➤ Each time you use a Calming Action technique, write a word or two to describe the situation, then check which Calming Action it was and circle whether doing it made you feel much better, better, slightly better, the same, or worse.

➤ Use a different cue sheet each time you use a Calming Action.

Give each student a Calming Actions Cue Sheet for each day until the next session. Show students how to fold each page into quarters to expose a different sheet each day.

Putting It All Together: Role Playing

AGENDA

1. Scanning Relaxation
2. Review of Session 7/Motivational Activity
3. Role playing of Calm Body/Clear Mind and Calming Actions
4. Home Practice

   Scanning Relaxation with rating sheet at least twice a week

   As needed: Quick Body Scanning in various settings; Calm Body, Clear Mind and Calming Actions with cue sheets

MATERIALS

➤ Student Manuals

➤ Scanning Relaxation CD and CD player

➤ Scanning Relaxation Rating Sheets

➤ Calm Body, Clear Mind Cue Sheets

➤ Calming Actions Cue Sheets

OBJECTIVES

Students will . . .

1. Review the main concepts presented in Session 7: Calming Actions.
2. Be able to provide specific examples of the use of the Calming Actions and discuss benefits of and difficulties in employing these actions.
3. Be able to employ the Calm Body, Clear Mind techniques and Calming Actions when role playing situations that have the potential to cause distress.

PROCEDURE

Scanning Relaxation

It's been a while since we did Scanning Relaxation with the CD, so let's start with that today.

Conduct Scanning Relaxation with the CD, following the procedures in Session 1. Have students fill out a Scanning Relaxation Rating Sheet before and after practice. Collect these and any rating sheets from home practice, and address any questions or comments. Answer any questions about students' use of Quick Body Scanning.

Review of Session 7/Motivational Activity

Who would like to share a time when you used **CALMING ACTIONS** since we last met? Let's take each Calming Action, one at a time. Who would like to share a time when you let feelings out?

Discuss this and the other four Calming Actions: talk about feelings, exercise, rest, and use distraction. Encourage each student to share at least one experience and to describe the results.

Turn to **page 43** in your manuals. Now that we've discussed the Calming Actions, think about the situation you just described, and check off what kind of Calming Action it was. Then take a minute to write a sentence or two to tell something about the situation.

If students did not practice a Calming Action or volunteer to describe one, ask them to imagine a time they might use one and write about that.

Who tried one of the Calming Actions but found that it didn't help reduce the upset feelings very much?

Troubleshoot; take suggestions for improvement from the other students. Collect any Calming Actions Cue Sheets the students have completed.

Role Playing of Calm Body, Clear Mind and Calming Actions

Life is full of stressful situations, but if you use your Calm Body, Clear Mind and Calming Actions techniques, you can reduce much of your distress. We are going to practice these techniques by role playing. This means we are going to act out situations that might cause you to feel upset or distressed.

*Refer students to the list of situations on **page 43** in their manuals.*

Today, we're going to help one another practice the Calm Body, Clear Mind techniques by doing some role plays. We'll also practice Calming Actions, if appropriate. Take a moment to look over the situations in your manuals. Would anyone like to role play one of these situations for the group?

Choose volunteers, and follow these general guidelines for conducting the role plays.

1. Choose a volunteer to be the main actor in the first role play.
2. Help the student choose any coactors the situation requires.

3. Give the actors a few minutes to discuss their parts in the role play. If necessary, help them determine how they will employ the Calm Body, Clear Mind techniques (and Calming Actions, if appropriate).

4. Instruct the main actor to "freeze frame" the action when he or she begins to feel tense or upset. First have the main actor use the Calm Body technique (if necessary, you can read the steps in Quick Body Scanning aloud while the main actor performs them). Then have the main actor go through the Clear Mind procedure aloud, illustrating self-talk with correct facts and correct meanings.

5. Ask the main actor whether any Calming Actions would be helpful and, if so, which ones.

6. Encourage the group to comment on the role play by asking the following questions:

➤ What happened in this situation?

➤ Has anything like this ever happened to you? If so, did you use the Calm Body, Clear Mind techniques? What about Calming Actions?

➤ How did using these techniques help _____ (the main actor) in this role play?

➤ Did _____ (the main actor) use any Calming Actions? If so, which ones? If not, would any Calming Actions help the person in this situation?

Role play as many situations as time permits.

Home Practice

*Refer students to **page 44** of their manuals, then go over the following instructions.*

1. Continue using the CD to practice Scanning Relaxation at least twice a week until the next meeting (more if desired). Fill out a Scanning Relaxation Rating Sheet *before* and *after* each practice.

Distribute Scanning Relaxation Rating Sheets.

2. Use Quick Body Scanning and the Calm Body, Clear Mind techniques as needed in various settings. Fill out a Calm Body, Clear Mind Cue Sheet each time you practice.

Distribute Calm Body, Clear Mind Cue Sheets.

3. Practice Calming Actions as needed. Each time you do, fill out a Calming Actions Cue Sheet.

Distribute the Calming Actions Cue Sheets.

Problem-Solving Actions

AGENDA

1. Quick Body Scanning
2. Review of Session 8/Motivational Activity
3. More behavioral coping: Problem-Solving Actions

   Identify the problem.

   Decide on your goal.

   List possible solutions.

   Figure out the consequences of each solution (long- and short-term consequences).

   Rate the consequences of each solution.
4. Problem Solver Worksheets
5. Home practice

   Scanning Relaxation with rating sheet at least twice a week before the next session (more if needed)

   As needed: Quick Body Scanning; Calm Body, Clear Mind; Calming Actions (cue sheets optional)

   Use of Problem Solver Worksheet at least once before the next session

MATERIALS

➤ Student Manuals

➤ Figure 13 (whole-class format; from Session 7)

➤ Figure 21 (reproduced in a whole-class format)

➤ Chalkboard, easel pad, overhead projector, or another whole-class format

➤ Scanning Relaxation Rating Sheets

➤ Optional: Calm Body, Clear Mind and Calming Actions Cue Sheets

➤ Problem Solver Worksheets

OBJECTIVES

Students will . . .

1. Review the Calm Body, Clear Mind and Calming Actions techniques.

2. Be able to describe specific examples of their use of the Calm Body, Clear Mind and Calming Actions techniques.

3. Be able to employ the five Problem-Solving Actions.

Quick Body Scanning

Have students practice Quick Body Scanning (read the complete script in Appendix A). Address any comments or questions about Scanning Relaxation home practice, then collect the Scanning Relaxation Rating Sheets. Answer any questions about students' use of Quick Body Scanning.

Review of Session 8/Motivational Activity

*Refer students to **page 45** in their manuals.*

Let's do a quick review.

➤ **CALM BODY** works by helping us relax muscle tension. What technique do we use to do this? *(Quick Body Scanning)*

➤ **CLEAR MIND** means we use correct self-talk. Self-talk has two parts. What are they? *(correct facts and correct meaning)*

➤ List the five **CALMING ACTIONS** *(let feelings out, talk about feelings, exercise, rest, use distraction)*

You've been using your Calm Body, Clear Mind techniques and the Calming Actions for some time now. Let's go around the group and share some situations and what happened when you used these techniques—how you felt before and after.

Start with a volunteer, and encourage everyone to speak. Collect the Calm Body, Clear Mind and Calming Actions Cue Sheets from home practice.

More Behavioral Coping: Problem-Solving Actions

Display the whole-class version of Figure 13.

1. Work out more feelings of tension and distress
2. Try to solve the problem

Figure 13

Earlier, we said that Calming Actions are things we could do to work out more feelings of tension and distress. We also said that there is another way to deal with the stress in our lives: Try to solve the problem.

Display the whole-class version of Figure 21.

PROBLEM-SOLVING ACTIONS
1. Identify the problem
2. Decide on your goal
3. List possible solutions
4. Figure out the consequences of each solution
5. Rate the consequences of each solution

Figure 21

PROBLEM-SOLVING ACTIONS work on the stressors or problem situations themselves. For example, if your best friend is mad at you, you can use the Calm Body, Clear Mind techniques, then plan ways to deal with the problem you and your friend are having. When you make this kind of plan, you are using Problem-Solving Actions.

Teaching you everything there is to know about problem solving would take more time than we have, so we're going to learn one general problem-solving process that you might find very useful.

The steps in this process and their descriptions are on **page 46** in your manuals.

Page 47 shows a worksheet you can use to help you figure out how to solve a problem. Follow along with the steps on **page 46** and the example on **page 47.** First put your name and the date at the top of the example page.

Step 1: Identify the problem
Decide what the problem (or stressor) is, and write it in the space at the top of the worksheet. Our example is *My hand is caught in a jar.*

Step 2: Decide on your goal

Decide how you would like things to be—what things would be like if your problem were solved. This is your *goal*. What is the goal in this example? *(Get my hand out of the jar.)* The goal is written on the line just below the problem.

Step 3: List possible solutions

Let your mind be free to think of as many solutions to the problem and ways to reach your goal as possible, no matter how far out or crazy, without deciding whether they are good or bad ideas. Write these on the worksheet in the spaces under the heading *Ideas/solutions*. Notice that our example lists four possible ideas/solutions:

1. Break the jar.
2. Have a friend pull on the jar.
3. Put the jar over a fire to melt it.
4. Put soapy water in the jar.

There are two spaces left on the worksheet. Does anyone have any other ideas?

Add other ideas/solutions as students give them. One example might be to put oil or grease in the jar.

Step 4: Figure out the consequences of each solution

Look at your solutions, one by one, and decide what would happen if you actually used that solution. Be sure to consider *all* the consequences for each solution, both the ones that will happen right away and those that will happen later. What are the consequences of the first solution in our example?

As students give consequences, write them on the chalkboard, easel pad, or other whole-class format.

Step 5: Rate the consequences of each solution

Rate these solutions based on their consequences. How good is each solution in solving the problem and helping you reach your goal? Use the following rating scale: One is very good, two is good, three is fair, four is poor, and five is terrible.

Rating consequences is a little tricky. If your idea solves one problem but creates another problem or has very negative consequences later, then you have to give the idea a lower rating.

For example, let's say you think your brother will eat your extra-large pepperoni pizza if you leave it in the refrigerator while you go to soccer practice. Eating the entire pizza before you leave solves that problem, but you will probably get very sick during the game and not play very well.

With the group, rate solutions for the sample problem.

Now let's try Problem-Solving Actions with another situation. Turn to **page 48** in your manuals, and fill out this worksheet as we discuss. Put your name and date at the top.

> ➤ *Step 1: Identify the problem.* (You forgot your lunch, and you are now hungry.)

> ➤ *Step 2: Decide on your goal.* (To get something to eat.)

> ➤ *Step 3: List possible solutions.*

Have the group suggest the solutions. Display their ideas in the whole-class format while students record them on their worksheets.

> ➤ *Step 4: Figure out the consequences of each solution.* Let's look at each idea and list the consequences (what would happen if we actually used the solution).

Have the group come up with the consequences. While you write these in the whole-class format, have students copy them onto their worksheets.

> ➤ *Step 5: Rate the consequences of each solution.* Look at the scale at the bottom of the worksheet: one means the consequences are very good, two is good, three is fair, four is poor, and five is terrible.

Have the group rate the solutions aloud, and record their ratings.

What do our ratings tell us are good and bad ideas or solutions? Remember, the lower the number, the better. We're looking for the "number one" solution.

Discuss until the group reaches a consensus.

Now look at **page 49** in your manuals for a harder problem. In this example, you were supposed to pick up concert tickets for yourself and your friend, but you forgot, and by the time you remembered, all the tickets were sold out. What is your problem?

Have a volunteer read the problem. Go through all the steps for the example. The two ideas already listed give the group an opportunity to evaluate poor solutions.

Point out that, although both of these solutions may have immediate positive consequences, they probably will have terrible consequences later on. For example, the friend might find out about the lie and get mad, and the people you stole the tickets from might come to the concert anyway and demand to sit in their seats.

Now fill in the Problem Solver Worksheet on **page 50** of your manuals with a problem you really have. You can do this in pairs.

Help students form pairs, then offer assistance as needed. When a pair is finished, ask them if you may read their situation, ideas/solutions, and consequences aloud, and let the group comment and give suggestions if necessary. Have extra worksheets available in case students need them.

Remember, using Calm Body, Clear Mind and Calming Actions will help you feel calm enough and clear enough in your thinking to use Problem-Solving Actions.

Home Practice

*Refer students to **page 51** of the Student Manual, and go over the following instructions.*

1. Continue to practice Scanning Relaxation with the CD at least twice a week before the next session (more if desired). Use a Scanning Relaxation Rating Sheet *before* and *after* each practice.

Distribute Scanning Relaxation Rating Sheets.

2. Use Quick Body Scanning; Calm Body, Clear Mind; and Calming Actions in various settings as needed.

If you wish, distribute Calm Body, Clear Mind and Calming Actions Cue Sheets.

3. Use the Problem Solver Worksheet at least once a week before the next session to help you learn the problem-solving steps.

Distribute Problem Solver Worksheets.

Personal Tension Spots/ General Review

AGENDA

1. Quick Body Scanning
2. Review of Session 9/Motivational Activity
3. Differential relaxation: Personal tension spots
4. General Review: Relaxation Bingo
5. Home Practice

   Scanning Relaxation with rating sheet at least twice a week before the next session (more if needed)

   As needed: Quick Body Scanning; Calm Body, Clear Mind; Calming Actions (cue sheets optional)

   Use of Problem Solver Worksheet at least once a week before the next session

MATERIALS

➤ Student Manuals

➤ Chalkboard, easel pad, overhead projector, or another whole-class format

➤ Figure 22 (reproduced in a whole-class format)

➤ Small pieces of candy (25 pieces for each student; M & M's, Reese's Pieces, Skittles, or the like)

➤ Scanning Relaxation Rating Sheets

➤ Optional: Calm Body, Clear Mind and Calming Actions Cue Sheets

➤ Problem Solver Worksheets

OBJECTIVES

Students will . . .

1. Review and demonstrate understanding of Session 9 by discussing their use of the Problem Solver Worksheet for one personal problem and by giving feedback to other students about their problem-solving efforts.
2. Be able to identify personal tension spots.

3. Be able to employ differential relaxation for personal tension spots.

4. Demonstrate knowledge of the major concepts of the program by providing correct answers during the Relaxation Bingo review.

PROCEDURE

Quick Body Scanning

Have students practice Quick Body Scanning (read the complete script in Appendix A). Address any comments or questions about Scanning Relaxation home practice, then collect Scanning Relaxation Rating Sheets and any Calm Body, Clear Mind or Calming Actions Cue Sheets. Answer any questions about students' use of these relaxation techniques.

Review of Session 9/Motivational Activity

*Refer students to **page 53** in their manuals.*

In the last session, you learned a way to deal directly with problems: Problem-Solving Actions. Everyone was going to try to use the Problem Solver Worksheet. Let's discuss how things went for you with Problem-Solving Actions.

Encourage the group to share their experiences, and write examples on the chalkboard, easel pad, or other whole-class format. Give feedback, and encourage students to give feedback, too. Collect the Problem Solver Worksheets.

Differential Relaxation: Personal Tension Spots

Since sessions began, you have learned two relaxation techniques. First, by using the CD, you learned to use Scanning Relaxation to relax muscle groups. Next you learned Quick Body Scanning. You've been practicing these techniques for quite a while now.

The last and fastest way to relax the body is sometimes called "differential relaxation." This means relaxing only certain parts of the body and not others.

While you have been doing Scanning Relaxation with the CD and filling out the Scanning Relaxation Rating Sheets, you've probably noticed that you have more tension in some areas than in others.

Display Figure 22.

PERSONAL TENSION SPOTS

Figure 22

These areas are called **PERSONAL TENSION SPOTS.** Personal tension spots are areas of your body where you hold the most tension.

It's not always necessary to scan your entire body to keep a Calm Body. To keep body tension down during the day, and especially to cope with False Alarms, it's often enough to scan and relax just these personal tension spots while keeping the rest of the body alert.

*Give an example of a couple of your own personal tension spots— for example, neck and shoulders or lower back. Ask students to list their personal tension spots on **page 53** in their manuals. (They should probably have only two or three.)*

Let's try relaxing our personal tension spots together right now. We'll say, **CALM BODY,** then breathe slowly and let go of the tension in each personal tension spot, one at a time.

Let's begin: Calm Body . . . inhale . . . exhale . . . relax and let go . . . and feel the relaxation entering the tension spot.

Pause to give students time to relax the first spot. Repeat for one or two more tension spots, then encourage discussion.

General Review: Relaxation Bingo

The purpose of Relaxation Bingo is to review important program concepts. It is not important to get five across, down, or diagonally, as it would be in regular bingo.

Now we're going to review all the different things we've learned during our sessions by playing a game of Relaxation Bingo.

➤ Turn to **page 54** in your manuals. This is your Relaxation Bingo board.

➤ I'm going to read some statements. Each statement has a certain word or words missing.

➤ You will write the missing word(s) in each statement on the correct square. For example, if I say "R1," this means you write the missing word(s) in the first column of the first row.

➤ These words are listed at the top of the page in alphabetical order. Cross the words out as you use them.

➤ After you write an answer in a square, put a piece of candy on top of it. If your answer is correct when we check it, you get to eat the candy right away.

➤ If your answer is not correct, you can eat the candy after you write the correct answer on the blank line for that square on **pages 55** and **56.**

Give each student 25 pieces of candy, one for each space. Follow these instructions to conduct the game. Statements and answers appear on the following pages in this guide.

1. Read the statement for each square.

2. After everyone writes the answer, ask the group what the correct answer is.

3. Prompt students who did not answer correctly to write the correct answer on the appropriate line.

4. Continue until you have read all the statements.

5. Ask students to total the number of items they left blank on the fill-in-the-blanks pages and write that number in the space for total correct.

Following the bingo game, let students know that the next session will be the last. Tell them that at this session you will serve refreshments, do some more review, and have them fill out some questionnaires.

Home Practice

*Refer students to **page 57** of the Student Manual, and go over the following instructions.*

1. Continue to practice Scanning Relaxation with the CD at least twice a week before the next session (more if desired). Use a Scanning Relaxation Rating Sheet *before* and *after* each practice.

Distribute Scanning Relaxation Rating Sheets.

2. Do Quick Body Scanning; Calm Body, Clear Mind; and Calming Actions in various settings as needed.

If you wish, distribute Calm Body, Clear Mind and Calming Actions Cue Sheets.

3. Use the Problem Solver Worksheet at least once a week before the next (and final) session to help you apply the problem-solving steps.

Distribute Problem Solver Worksheets.

Relaxation Bingo Statements and Answers

R1: _____ _____ is the cue we use to put our bodies into relaxation. *(Calm Body)*

E1: Pacing the floor, biting your fingernails, clenching your jaw, perspiring palms, and tense muscles are all signs of _____. *(stress)*

L1: _____ trigger our stress reactions. *(Stressors)*

A1: We often react to a stressor by tensing our _____ . *(muscles)*

X1: Harmful stress is called _____ . *(distress)*

R2: If you have an emergency reaction to something that is really *not* a danger, this is a _____ Alarm. *(False)*

E2: Distress over a long period of time can cause _____. *(illness)*

L2: We used a CD to learn how to relax all the muscles in our bodies. This is called _____ _____ . *(Scanning Relaxation)*

A2: We call the amount of stress and distress a person feels comfortable dealing with the person's _____ _____ . *(comfort zone)*

X2: Stress enters my body through my _____ . *(mind)*

R3: Quick thoughts or images (mental pictures) we have when we experience a stressor are called _____ _____ . *(automatic thoughts)*

E3: Something is a stressor if we think it is a _____ or threat to us. *(danger)*

L3: A quick way to relax all the muscles in your body is called _____ _____ _____ . *(Quick Body Scanning)*

A3: To make sure our self-talk is correct, we use the _____ _____ cue. *(Clear Mind)*

X3: Yelling and crying are just some of the many ways to let _____ out. *(feelings)*

R4: Sometimes a stressful situation leaves us so tired that the best thing to do is to _____ for a while. *(rest)*

E4: In the Clear Mind technique, you check for correct facts and correct _____. *(meaning)*

L4: In contrast to relaxing, an active way of working out the tension in our muscles is by doing some _____ . *(exercise)*

A4: If incorrect thoughts or pictures keep popping into your mind, it may be helpful to keep your mind busy with _____ . *(distractions)*

X4: It sometimes helps to reduce our stress if we _____ to someone about our feelings. *(talk)*

R5: Sometimes we can work on the stressor itself by using Problem-_____ Actions. *(Solving)*

E5: Instead of relaxing all of our muscles, we can relax just the areas where we carry most of our tension. These are called _____ _____ spots. *(personal tension)*

L5: After we decide on a problem, the next step is to decide the way we'd like it to be. This is called a _____ . *(goal)*

A5: To take care of a problem or achieve a goal, we try to come up with as many _____ as possible. *(solutions)*

X5: To decide which are the best solutions, you need to figure out the _____ of each and rate them. *(consequences)*

General Review/Program Evaluation

AGENDA

1. Scanning Relaxation
2. Review of Session 10
3. General review/Motivational Activity
4. Evaluation and student feedback

MATERIALS

➤ Student Manuals
➤ Scanning Relaxation CD and CD player
➤ Refreshments
➤ Program evaluation measures (from Appendix D)
➤ Certificates of Achievement (from Appendix B)

PROCEDURE

Scanning Relaxation

Conduct Scanning Relaxation with the CD, following the procedures in Session 1. Have students fill out a Scanning Relaxation Rating Sheet before and after practice. Collect these and any cue sheets from home practice, and address questions or comments about students' use of the relaxation techniques.

Review of Session 10

*Share the refreshments. Direct students to **page 59** in the Student Manual, and congratulate them for having worked hard and completed the program.*

This page lists all the relaxation and stress-management techniques you have learned during this program. Who would like to share some experiences using any of these techniques? What about relaxing personal tension spots?

Have each volunteer present his or her experiences very briefly, followed by group reactions. Collect the Problem Solver Worksheets students completed as home practice for Session 10.

General Review/Motivational Activity

To review all we've learned so far, I'm going to have you complete the Stress Management Crossword Puzzle on **pages 60** and **61** of your manuals.

After students have finished the puzzle, go over the answers as a group. (Answers appear on the next page of this guide.) Briefly discuss any questions.

Evaluation and Student Feedback

Administer the program evaluation measures to the group. Collect these, then ask students to give an oral evaluation of specific program components. Sample questions follow.

Relaxation techniques

1. How do you feel about the Scanning Relaxation? Was the CD useful?
2. Were you able to practice the Scanning Relaxation regularly?
3. Which relaxation techniques did you find most helpful? Least helpful? Why?
4. How useful were the Scanning Relaxation Rating Sheets?

Student Manual and other materials

1. How did you feel about the Student Manual? Were the materials clearly written and useful?
2. Were the forms and worksheets helpful?

These were the Scanning Relaxation Rating Sheet; Steps in Quick Body Scanning page; False Alarm Sheet; Calm Body, Clear Mind Cue Sheet; Calming Actions Cue Sheet; and Problem Solver Worksheet.

Program content

1. Were the main ideas presented in a way that helped you understand them?
2. Were some terms or ideas difficult to understand? If so, what were they?

If you wish, ask the group to make general comments and suggestions for improving the program.

Hand out the Certificates of Achievement, then thank students for their participation, sharing, and time. Let them know they can keep their manuals, and encourage them to continue using the techniques they have learned in the sessions.

Stress Management Crossword Puzzle
Answer Key

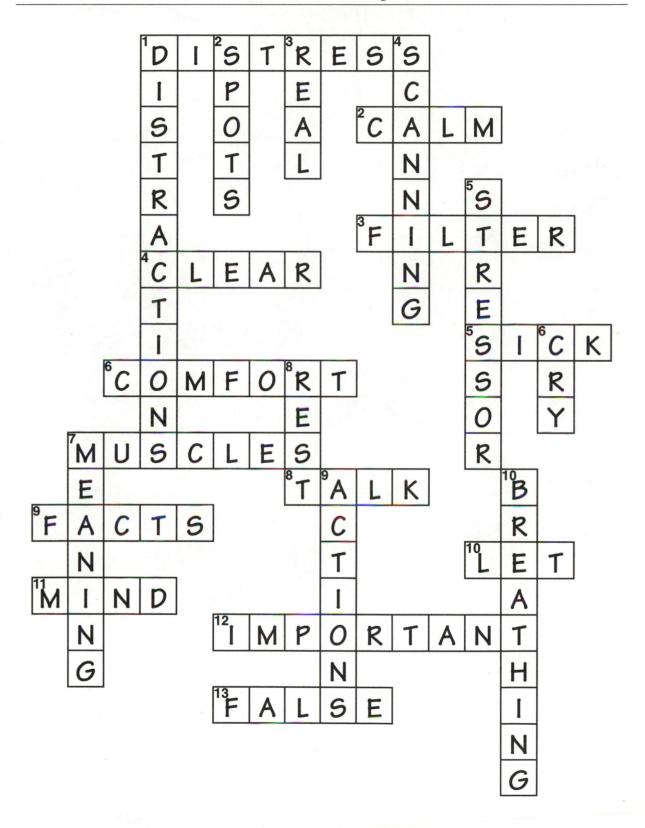

APPENDIX A

Relaxation Scripts

Scanning Relaxation Script

Use the boldface headings and italicized directives for reference only, and do not read them aloud. Indications to pause occur within most paragraphs. These pauses should be brief. Include a slightly longer pause between each paragraph.

PREPARATION

Now we're going to practice Scanning Relaxation. *(Pause.)*

Spend a little time getting as comfortable as you can. While you are finding a good position, you will also want to loosen any tight clothing. *(Pause.)* Loosen your shirt or blouse at the neck. *(Pause.)* Loosen your belt. *(Pause.)* If your shoes feel a little tight, then take them off. *(Pause.)* Allow your eyes to close.

Mentally, you should begin to clear your mind of the busyness and rushing that fill your life. Let a passive attitude develop. Try to let the relaxation begin.

Open your mouth for a moment, and move your jaw *slowly* and easily from side to side. *(Pause.)* Now let your mouth close, keeping your teeth slightly apart. As you do, breathing through your nose, take a deep breath *(pause)*, and then open your mouth slightly and slowly let the air slip out.

BREATHING

Take another deep breath. *(Pause.)* As you breathe out, silently say, "*Relax . . .* and let go." *(Pause.)* Feel yourself floating down. Now that you are comfortable, let yourself relax even further. The more you can let go, the better it will be.

Again, take a deep breath. *(Pause.)* As you breathe out, silently say, "*Relax . . .* and let go." Just let the air slip out easily and automatically, and already you may be feeling a little calmer. Now just carry on breathing normally.

Study your own body and the feelings you are experiencing. *(Pause.)* As you relax more and more, your breathing becomes slower. You may notice that it is slower now, and you breathe more and more from the bottom of your lungs.

It's too much trouble to move *(pause)*, just too much trouble to move. All tension is leaving you, and you are so very comfortable. Notice that you have a feeling of well-being, as though any troubles have been set aside, and nothing seems to matter.

BODY SCANNING

Now, as we continue, let's use the natural abilities of your mind and body to experience feelings of deep, deep relaxation. We will do this by going through your body from head to foot, spreading those good feelings of relaxation. Each time you breathe out, you should feel more relaxed.

Keep your eyes gently closed. Relax your jaw muscles. Keep your teeth slightly apart and your face, neck, and shoulders loose and relaxed.

As you think about each part of your body and you allow that part of your body to relax, you will feel all the tension flowing away, and that part of your body will be comfortable *(pause)*, calm *(pause)*, and peaceful. Each time you breathe out, you will become more relaxed and feel the relaxation spreading slowly through your body.

HEAD AND NECK SCANNING

Now think about the top of your head. Feel the area. As you breathe out, feel the top of your head relax more and more, as it becomes loose and free of wrinkles. Let the tensions flow from the top of your head. The top of your head is becoming completely relaxed.

Think of your forehead. Feel it, the skin that covers it. Feel your eyes, the muscles that are around them. Feel those muscles relaxing more and more with each breath. Feel your forehead relaxing more and more.

Your eyelids grow heavier and quieter with each breath. Let yourself go as you breathe gently in and out. Let the relaxation spread naturally as the tension flows out each time you exhale. Your forehead *(pause)*, your eyes *(pause)*, and all these muscles are relaxing more and more.

Feel your throat and neck. Feel them relax. As you breathe out, you *"Relax . . . and let go."* Your throat and neck are loose, quiet, and comfortable.

SHOULDERS AND ARMS SCANNING

Feel your shoulders and upper back. Be aware of the skin and muscles of your shoulders and upper back. *(Pause.)* Effortlessly, allow relaxation to spread into your shoulders and upper back. *(Pause.)* With each breath you take, each time you breathe out, you become *more* and *more* relaxed. *(Pause.)* The muscles are loose and comfortable. Feel quiet in your shoulder muscles.

Feel your upper arms relaxing. Feel your arms and hands. Your arms, hands, and fingers are feeling *very, very* relaxed. You may feel warmth or tingling in your arms and hands. *(Pause.)* Feel your arms, hands, and fingers relaxing. Feel the tension dropping from your arms, hands, and fingers.

CHEST AND STOMACH SCANNING

Now think about your chest. Feel it. Sense the muscles under the skin around the chest. Be deeply aware of your chest. Feel relaxation spreading throughout your chest and stomach area. *(Pause.)* As you breathe out, feel the *calm* and relaxation in your chest. As you breathe naturally, feel relaxation and quiet in your chest and in your stomach area. Tension flows out from your chest as you breathe out.

Breathing in and breathing out. More and more, you feel calm. *(Pause.)* Feel your stomach. Be aware of the skin and muscles in this area. Feel these muscles relax. Feel the tension being replaced by pleasant relaxation. As you breathe out, feel relaxation spread to your stomach and lower back.

HIPS AND LEGS SCANNING

Now feel your hips, your legs, your thighs, your calves, and your ankles. Be aware of these parts of your body. Feel the muscles in these areas. Allow them to relax more and more. *(Pause.)* Let calm flow down into your legs. Feel the tension leaving. Your hips, thighs, calves, and ankles are becoming loose and relaxed.

Feel your feet and your toes. Become deeply aware of your feet and each toe. Feel how still and relaxed they are. Let all the tension leave your feet and toes.

BODY REVIEW SCANNING

What does your body feel like? Is it tingly? Is it heavy? Does it feel hollow? Does it feel light, as if you were floating? What does your body feel like?

Become aware of the tiniest feelings and try to describe these feelings to yourself. *(Pause.)* Now, for about thirty seconds or so, scan your body for any signs of tension. If you find any tension in any muscle group, let it slip out. Try to let the tension flow out and the relaxation flow in to take its place.

Think about the ocean as you continue to scan your body for tension. Imagine that each wave that rolls in brings with it massaging and gentle relaxation and calmness. As the wave rolls out, it pulls along with it any tension that remains in your body. Scan your body. *(Pause.)* If you find any tension, let it go.

MASSAGING RELAXATION

Go through your body once more, and relax even more until a very deep relaxation finds its place everywhere in your body.

Picture the ocean waves rolling in and out with each breath. And with each breath imagine gently massaging relaxation flowing all over your body.

Conclusion

Now think to yourself how very relaxed you feel. Soon you will get up and continue with your day. As you go about your daily activities, try to carry this deep feeling of relaxation with you. Remember, anytime you feel the need, you can put yourself back into relaxation by saying, *"Relax . . . and let go."*

Quick Body Scanning Script

Use the boldface headings and italicized directives for reference only, and do not read them aloud.

SHOULDERS AND ARMS

As you breathe in, scan your shoulders and arms *(Pause.)* As you breathe out, feel the tension slip away. Arms and shoulders relax. Once again, as you breathe in, attend to your shoulders, arms, and hands. *(Pause.)* As you breathe out, your relaxation is becoming deeper and deeper.

CHEST AND LUNGS

As you breathe in, scan your chest and lungs. *(Pause.)* As you breathe out, feel the tension slip away. Chest and lungs relax. Once again, as you breathe in, attend to your chest and lungs. *(Pause.)* As you breathe out, your relaxation is becoming deeper and deeper.

STOMACH AREA

As you breathe in, scan your stomach area. *(Pause.)* As you breathe out, feel the tension slip away. Stomach area relax. Once again, as you breathe in, attend to your stomach area. *(Pause.)* As you breathe out, your relaxation is becoming deeper and deeper.

LEGS AND FEET

As you breathe in, scan your legs and feet. *(Pause.)* As you breathe out, feel the tension slip away. Legs and feet relax. Once again, as you breathe in, scan your hips, legs, and feet. *(Pause.)* As you breathe out, your relaxation is becoming deeper and deeper. Now allow your breathing to become smooth and rhythmic.

RETURN TO ACTIVITY

Let your body continue to relax as you return to your daily activities. Continue to feel calm and at ease. *(Pause.)* If at any time during your day you begin to feel tense or uptight, scan your body to find the tension and then relax and let go with each breath.

Program Forms

Scanning Relaxation Rating Sheet

Name _____ **Date** _____

Check one: _____ Before practice   _____ After practice

Rate your feelings of relaxation from 1 (very relaxed) to 5 (very tense) for each muscle group. Circle your rating for each group. Then add these ratings to get a total score.

Forehead and eyes

very relaxed _____ very tense

    1   2   3   4   5

Jaws and mouth

very relaxed _____ very tense

    1   2   3   4   5

Neck

very relaxed _____ very tense

    1   2   3   4   5

Shoulders

very relaxed _____ very tense

    1   2   3   4   5

Arms and hands

very relaxed _____ very tense

    1   2   3   4   5

Chest

very relaxed _____ very tense

    1   2   3   4   5

Back

very relaxed _____ very tense

    1   2   3   4   5

Stomach

very relaxed _____ very tense

    1   2   3   4   5

Hips

very relaxed _____ very tense

    1   2   3   4   5

Legs and feet

very relaxed _____ very tense

    1   2   3   4   5

TOTAL _____

False Alarm Sheet

Name _____ **Date** _____

1. Stressor (What happened?)

_____

_____

_____

2. Self-talk

_____

_____

_____

3. Meaning (Why is this important to me?)

_____

_____

_____

4. Physiological (body) reactions

_____

_____

_____

Steps in Quick Body Scanning

1. As you breathe in, scan your face, neck, shoulders, and arms.

2. As you breathe out, feel any tension slip away.

3. As you breathe in, scan your chest, lungs, and stomach.

4. As you breathe out, feel any tension slip away.

5. As you breathe in, scan your hips, legs, and feet.

6. As you breathe out, feel any tension slip away.

Calm Body, Clear Mind

Name _____   Date _____

1. Situation: _____

   much better   better   slightly better   the same   worse

2. Situation: _____

   much better   better   slightly better   the same   worse

3. Situation: _____

   much better   better   slightly better   the same   worse

Calm Body, Clear Mind

Name _____   Date _____

1. Situation: _____

   much better   better   slightly better   the same   worse

2. Situation: _____

   much better   better   slightly better   the same   worse

3. Situation: _____

   much better   better   slightly better   the same   worse

Calm Body, Clear Mind

Name _____   Date _____

1. Situation: _____

   much better   better   slightly better   the same   worse

2. Situation: _____

   much better   better   slightly better   the same   worse

3. Situation: _____

   much better   better   slightly better   the same   worse

Calm Body, Clear Mind

Name _____   Date _____

1. Situation: _____

   much better   better   slightly better   the same   worse

2. Situation: _____

   much better   better   slightly better   the same   worse

3. Situation: _____

   much better   better   slightly better   the same   worse

Calming Actions

Name _____ **Date** _____

Situation _____

☐ **Let feelings out**
much better | better | slightly better | the same | worse

☐ **Talk about feelings**
much better | better | slightly better | the same | worse

☐ **Exercise**
much better | better | slightly better | the same | worse

☐ **Rest**
much better | better | slightly better | the same | worse

☐ **Use distraction**
much better | better | slightly better | the same | worse

Calming Actions

Name _____ **Date** _____

Situation _____

☐ **Let feelings out**
much better | better | slightly better | the same | worse

☐ **Talk about feelings**
much better | better | slightly better | the same | worse

☐ **Exercise**
much better | better | slightly better | the same | worse

☐ **Rest**
much better | better | slightly better | the same | worse

☐ **Use distraction**
much better | better | slightly better | the same | worse

Calming Actions

Name _____ **Date** _____

Situation _____

☐ **Let feelings out**
much better | better | slightly better | the same | worse

☐ **Talk about feelings**
much better | better | slightly better | the same | worse

☐ **Exercise**
much better | better | slightly better | the same | worse

☐ **Rest**
much better | better | slightly better | the same | worse

☐ **Use distraction**
much better | better | slightly better | the same | worse

Calming Actions

Name _____ **Date** _____

Situation _____

☐ **Let feelings out**
much better | better | slightly better | the same | worse

☐ **Talk about feelings**
much better | better | slightly better | the same | worse

☐ **Exercise**
much better | better | slightly better | the same | worse

☐ **Rest**
much better | better | slightly better | the same | worse

☐ **Use distraction**
much better | better | slightly better | the same | worse

Problem Solver Worksheet

Name _____ **Date** _____

Problem _____

Goal _____

Ideas/solutions	Consequences (now and later)	Rating
1.		
2.		
3.		
4.		
5.		
6.		

Ratings

1 = very good   2 = good   3 = fair   4 = poor   5 = terrible

CERTIFICATE OF ACHIEVEMENT

_____

has completed the *Stress Management Program*

_____
SIGNATURE

_____
DATE

APPENDIX C

Figures

Figure 1

STRESS

STRESSORS

Figure 2

102

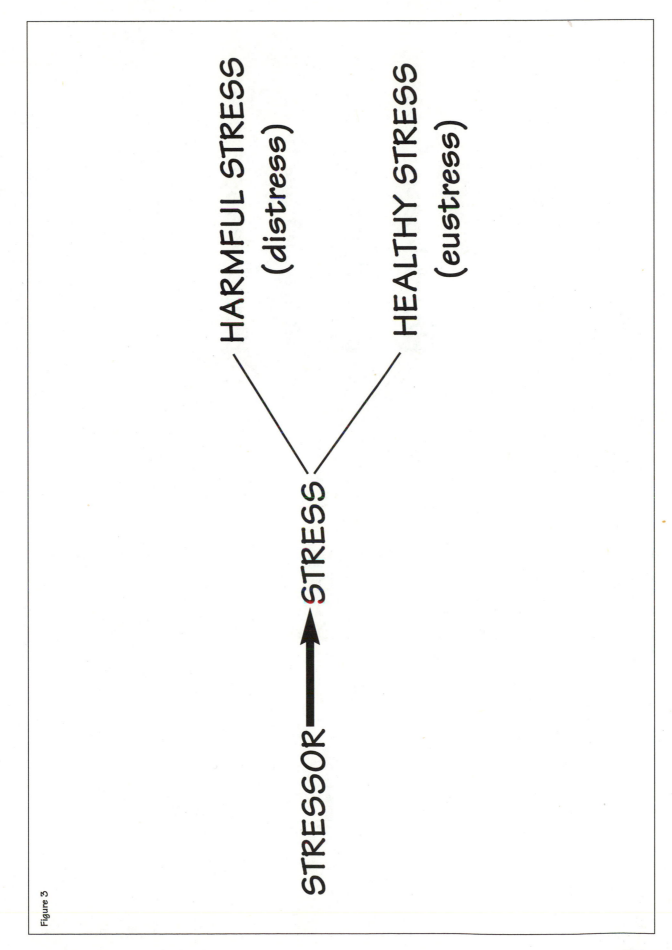

Figure 3

103

Figure 4

104

Figure 5

STRESSOR ➔ DISTRESS ➔ ILLNESS

Worrying about _____

Stomach acid released

Sensitive, burning stomach

COMFORT ZONE

Figure 6

106

STRESS FILTER

Figure 7

STRESS AND DISTRESS ENTER

MY BODY MY MIND THROUGH MY BODY MY MIND

Figure 8

108

DANGER
THREAT

Figure 9

SELF-TALK

Figure 10

110

Figure 11

CALM BODY
CLEAR MIND

CLEAR MIND = SELF TALK WITH

1. Correct facts

2. Correct meaning

Figure 12

112

Figure 13

1. Work out more feelings of tension and distress

2. Try to solve the problem

LET FEELINGS OUT

Figure 14

Figure 15

TALK ABOUT FEELINGS

EXERCISE

Figure 16

116

REST

Figure 17

CALMING ACTIONS

1. Let feelings out

2. Talk about feelings

3. Exercise

4. Rest

Figure 18

118

Figure 19

USE DISTRACTION

CALMING ACTIONS

1. Let feelings out
2. Talk about feelings
3. Exercise
4. Rest
5. Use distraction

Figure 20

120

Figure 21

PROBLEM-SOLVING ACTIONS

1. Identify the problem

2. Decide on your goal

3. List possible solutions

4. Figure out the consequences of each solution

5. Rate the consequences of each solution

Figure 22

PERSONAL TENSION SPOTS

Program Evaluation Measures

Pretests/Posttests

The following three measures can be used as pretests and posttests. All pretesting should be conducted prior to and *not* during the first session of the program. Posttesting should be conducted after Session 10, the final content session. Otherwise, program assessment should be flexible, with each program site selecting the measures most suitable to its particular treatment goals, setting, and staff time.

Stress Measure

The Stress Measure assesses the degree and frequency of adolescents' experience of stress in a typical day and a typical week. It also includes a global self-assessment of their ability to cope with the stress in their lives.

Coping Measure

There are two versions of the Coping Measure. Coping Measure I is designed to obtain information on the frequency and effectiveness of specific positive and negative coping strategies. Positive and negative items are intermingled in this version. Because in some nonclinical settings students may view identifying certain negative coping strategies as inappropriate or threatening, Coping Measure II separates positive from negative coping strategies, allowing students to choose whether or not to respond to the negative items. Both versions allow students to identify and rate up to five other stress management strategies they employ.

Understanding Stress

This measure assesses adolescents' knowledge of general concepts and principles presented in the program.

Progress and Posttest-Only Measures

The following additional progress and posttest-only measures assess the effectiveness of various skills taught in the program, including the Scanning Relaxation technique and cognitive and behavioral coping strategies.

Scanning Relaxation Data Record

Data obtained from the Scanning Relaxation Rating Sheets can show, over time, changes in the effectiveness of the Scanning Relaxation procedure.

Calm Body, Clear Mind and Calming Actions Data Records

These two data records offer a means of comparing a student's responses on the Calm Body, Clear Mind and Calming Actions Cue Sheets over time.

Relaxation Bingo and Stress Management Crossword Puzzle Scoring Formulas

These formulas reflect students' comprehension of the program's main concepts, as reflected by performance on the Relaxation Bingo game (Session 10) and the Stress Management Crossword Puzzle (Final Session).

REFERENCES

For further information about both the Stress Measure and the Coping Measure, see the following sources:

de Anda, D., with Baroni, S., Boskin, L., Buchwald, L., Morgan, J., Ow, J., Siegel Gold, J., & Weiss, R. (2000). Stress, stressors, and coping among high school students. *Children and Youth Services Review, 21*, 441–463.

de Anda, D., with Bradley, M., Collada, C., Dunn, L., Hollister, V., Kubota, J., Miltenberger, J., Pulley, J., Susskind, A., Thompson, L. A., & Wentworth, T. (1997). A study of stress, stressors, and coping strategies among middle school adolescents. *Social Work in Education, 19*(2), 97–98.

Stress Measure

Student _____ **Date** _____

Circle the answer to each statement below, using the following scale.

very often	often	not very often	never
4	3	2	1

1. During a *typical* day

   a. how often do you feel a *little* stressed? | 4 3 2 1

   b. how often do you feel *very* stressed? | 4 3 2 1

2. During a *typical* week

   a. how often do you feel a *little* stressed? | 4 3 2 1

   b. how often do you feel *very* stressed? | 4 3 2 1

3. How often do you feel you can handle stressful | 4 3 2 1
   or upsetting situations?

In general, how well do you feel you cope with the stress in your life? *(Circle one.)*

very well	fairly well	OK	not very well	not well at all

Coping Measure I

Circle the number that shows how often you do the following things (a) and how much you think they help you (b). Use the following scale.

very often	often	not very often	never
4	3	2	1

When I am feeling stressed and upset . . .

1. a.	I try to make my body relax.	4	3	2	1
b.	This helps me feel less stressed.	4	3	2	1
2. a.	I do something to distract myself like watch TV or listen to music.	4	3	2	1
b.	This helps me feel less stressed.	4	3	2	1
3. a.	I overeat.	4	3	2	1
b.	This helps me feel less stressed.	4	3	2	1
4. a.	I rest for short periods of time.	4	3	2	1
b.	This helps me feel less stressed.	4	3	2	1
5. a.	I use drugs and/or alcohol.	4	3	2	1
b.	This helps me feel less stressed.	4	3	2	1
6. a.	I smoke cigarettes.	4	3	2	1
b.	This helps me feel less stressed.	4	3	2	1
7. a.	I do something physical like exercise or sports.	4	3	2	1
b.	This helps me feel less stressed.	4	3	2	1
8. a.	I yell at other people.	4	3	2	1
b.	This helps me feel less stressed.	4	3	2	1
9. a.	I talk to someone about my feelings.	4	3	2	1
b.	This helps me feel less stressed.	4	3	2	1
10. a.	I try to figure out how to change things or solve the problem.	4	3	2	1
b.	This helps me feel less stressed.	4	3	2	1
11. a.	I destroy and break things.	4	3	2	1
b.	This helps me feel less stressed.	4	3	2	1
12. a.	I try to think about the situation differently.	4	3	2	1
b.	This helps me feel less stressed.	4	3	2	1

	very often 4	often 3	not very often 2	never 1
13. a. I fight (physically) with others.	4	3	2	1
b. This helps me feel less stressed.	4	3	2	1
14. a. I tell myself I'm really not upset.	4	3	2	1
b. This helps me feel less stressed.	4	3	2	1
15. a. I try to make sure I understand the situation.	4	3	2	1
b. This helps me feel less stressed.	4	3	2	1
16. a. I daydream and pretend things are different.	4	3	2	1
b. This helps me feel less stressed.	4	3	2	1
17. a. I let my feelings out.	4	3	2	1
b. This helps me feel less stressed.	4	3	2	1
18. a. I slow my breathing and try to calm down.	4	3	2	1
b. This helps me feel less stressed.	4	3	2	1
19. a. I try to hurt myself physically.	4	3	2	1
b. This helps me feel less stressed.	4	3	2	1
20. a. I pull away from people by sleeping a lot or staying in my room.	4	3	2	1
b. This helps me feel less stressed.	4	3	2	1

List any other things you do to deal with stress. Circle the number from 1 to 4 that shows how often you do these things (a) and how much you think they help you (b).

When I am feeling stressed and upset . . .

21. a. _____	4	3	2	1
b. This helps me feel less stressed.	4	3	2	1
22. a. _____	4	3	2	1
b. This helps me feel less stressed.	4	3	2	1
23. a. _____	4	3	2	1
b. This helps me feel less stressed.	4	3	2	1
24. a. _____	4	3	2	1
b. This helps me feel less stressed.	4	3	2	1
25. a. _____	4	3	2	1
b. This helps me feel less stressed.	4	3	2	1

Coping Measure I, page 2

Coping Measure I: Scoring Form

Total scores for items marked "a" provide information on the frequency with which the student employs positive or negative coping strategies. Total scores for items marked "b" indicate how effective the student considers the coping strategies to be. Responses to Items 21–25 are collected but not scored.

To obtain total scores for either positive coping strategies or negative coping strategies, sum the numeric ratings for each item in that category. Dividing these total scores by 10 (the number of positive and negative items, respectively) will convert the score to a value on the 4-point scale:

very often	often	not very often	never
4	3	2	1

Positive Coping Strategies

Items 1, 2, 4, 7, 9, 10, 12, 15, 17, 18

Total scores

(sum of "a" answers) $\dfrac{\rule{2cm}{0.4pt}}{10}$ = _____ (frequency rate)

(sum of "b" answers) $\dfrac{\rule{2cm}{0.4pt}}{10}$ = _____ (effectiveness rate)

Negative Coping Strategies

Items 3, 5, 6, 8, 11, 13, 14, 16, 19, 20

Total scores

(sum of "a" answers) $\dfrac{\rule{2cm}{0.4pt}}{10}$ = _____ (frequency rate)

(sum of "b" answers) $\dfrac{\rule{2cm}{0.4pt}}{10}$ = _____ (effectiveness rate)

Coping Measure II

PART A

Student _____ **Date** _____

Circle the number that shows how often you do the following things (a) and how much you think they help you (b). Using the following scale.

very often	often	not very often	never
4	3	2	1

When I am feeling stressed and upset . . .

1. a. I try to make my body relax.	4	3	2	1
b. This helps me feel less stressed.	4	3	2	1
2. a. I do something to distract myself like watch TV or listen to music.	4	3	2	1
b. This helps me feel less stressed.	4	3	2	1
3. a. I rest for short periods of time.	4	3	2	1
b. This helps me feel less stressed.	4	3	2	1
4. a. I do something physical like exercise or sports.	4	3	2	1
b. This helps me feel less stressed.	4	3	2	1
5. a. I talk to someone about my feelings.	4	3	2	1
b. This helps me feel less stressed.	4	3	2	1
6. a. I try to figure out how to change things or solve the problem.	4	3	2	1
b. This helps me feel less stressed.	4	3	2	1
7. a. I try to think about the situation differently.	4	3	2	1
b. This helps me feel less stressed.	4	3	2	1
8. a. I try to make sure I understand the situation.	4	3	2	1
b. This helps me feel less stressed.	4	3	2	1
9. a. I let my feelings out.	4	3	2	1
b. This helps me feel less stressed.	4	3	2	1
10. a. I slow my breathing and try to calm down.	4	3	2	1
b. This helps me feel less stressed.	4	3	2	1

PART B

You can choose to skip items 11 through 20 if you wish.

very often	often	not very often	never
4	3	2	1

When I am feeling stressed and upset . . .

	very often	often	not very often	never
11. a. I overeat.	4	3	2	1
b. This helps me feel less stressed.	4	3	2	1
12. a. I use drugs and/or alcohol.	4	3	2	1
b. This helps me feel less stressed.	4	3	2	1
13. a. I smoke cigarettes.	4	3	2	1
b. This helps me feel less stressed.	4	3	2	1
14. a. I yell at other people.	4	3	2	1
b. This helps me feel less stressed.	4	3	2	1
15. a. I destroy and break things.	4	3	2	1
b. This helps me feel less stressed.	4	3	2	1
16. a. I fight (physically) with others.	4	3	2	1
b. This helps me feel less stressed.	4	3	2	1
17. a. I tell myself I'm really not upset.	4	3	2	1
b. This helps me feel less stressed.	4	3	2	1
18. a. I daydream and pretend things are different.	4	3	2	1
b. This helps me feel less stressed.	4	3	2	1
19. a. I try to hurt myself physically.	4	3	2	1
b. This helps me feel less stressed.	4	3	2	1
20. a. I pull away from people by sleeping a lot or staying in my room.	4	3	2	1
b. This helps me feel less stressed.	4	3	2	1

List any other things you do to deal with stress. Circle the number from 1 to 4 that shows how often you do these things (a) and how much they think they help you (b).

When I am feeling stressed and upset . . .

	very often	often	not very often	never
21. a. _____	4	3	2	1
b. This helps me feel less stressed.	4	3	2	1
22. a. _____	4	3	2	1
b. This helps me feel less stressed.	4	3	2	1
23. a. _____	4	3	2	1
b. This helps me feel less stressed.	4	3	2	1
24. a. _____	4	3	2	1
b. This helps me feel less stressed.	4	3	2	1
25. a. _____	4	3	2	1
b. This helps me feel less stressed.	4	3	2	1

Coping Measure II, page 2

Coping Measure II: Scoring Form

Part A: Positive Coping Strategies

Total scores for Items 1–10 marked "a" provide information on the frequency with which the student employs positive coping strategies. Total scores for items marked "b" indicate how effective the student considers the coping strategies to be.

To obtain total scores for positive coping strategies (Items 1–10), sum the numeric ratings for each item in that category. Dividing these total scores by 10 (the number of positive items) will convert the score to a value on the 4-point scale:

very often	often	not very often	never
4	3	2	1

Total scores

(sum of "a" answers) $\dfrac{\rule{2cm}{0.4pt}}{10}$ = _____ (frequency rate)

(sum of "b" answers) $\dfrac{\rule{2cm}{0.4pt}}{10}$ = _____ (effectiveness rate)

Part B: Negative Coping Strategies

Total scores for Items 11–20 marked "a" provide information on the frequency with which the student employs negative coping strategies. Total scores for items marked "b" indicate how effective the student considers the coping strategies to be.

To obtain total scores for negative coping strategies (Items 11-20), sum the numeric ratings for each item in that category. Dividing these total scores by 10 (the number of negative items) will convert the score to a value on the 4-point scale:

very often	often	not very often	never
4	3	2	1

Total scores

(sum of "a" answers) $\dfrac{\rule{2cm}{0.4pt}}{10}$ = _____ (frequency rate)

(sum of "b" answers) $\dfrac{\rule{2cm}{0.4pt}}{10}$ = _____ (effectiveness rate)

Responses to Items 21–25 are collected but not scored.

Understanding Stress

Student _____ **Date** _____

Circle "T" if the statement is true and "F" if the statement is false.

T F   1. To be healthy, you need to remove all the stress from your life.

T F   2. Your thoughts can cause you to feel stressed.

T F   3. Stress is a natural response to danger or threat.

T F   4. Talking to someone about your feelings can help reduce your stress.

T F   5. Taking quick, short breaths will help you relax and calm down.

T F   6. Relaxing your muscles helps you feel less stressed.

T F   7. Stress over a long period of time can cause illness.

T F   8. Different people are comfortable with different amounts of stress.

T F   9. The way you *think* about something determines whether or not it is stressful for you.

T F 10. If you hold stress in and ignore it, it will go away.

Circle the letter of the correct or best answer.

11. When we are feeling stressed, our muscles become
    a. weak
    b. shaky
    c. painful
    d. tense and tight

12. Before we get upset about something, we should make sure that our understanding of _____ and _____ is correct.
    a. the time and place
    b. the facts and meaning
    c. people and things
    d. what is right and wrong

13. We can decide what is the best action to take to solve a problem that is upsetting us by
    a. flipping a coin
    b. following our feelings
    c. figuring out what the results or consequences of our actions will be
    d. asking our friends

14. The first thing we should do when we feel ourselves becoming stressed or upset is to
    a. yell and let out our feelings
    b. take a break for a few minutes and relax our muscles
    c. get away from everyone
    d. ignore the feeling until it goes away

15. Which of the following will *not* help reduce stress?

    a. exercise

    b. ignoring how we feel

    c. rest

    d. talking about how we feel

Understanding Stress: Scoring Formula

Answers

1–F	6–T	11–d
2–T	7–T	12–b
3–T	8–T	13–c
4–T	9–T	14–b
5–F	10–F	15–b

(total number correct) $\dfrac{\rule{2cm}{0.4pt}}{15} \times 100 = \rule{1.5cm}{0.4pt}$ (percentage correct)

Scanning Relaxation Data Record

Student _____ **Date** _____

Subtract the after score from the before score to obtain the gain score. Add the gain scores to obtain the total gain score.

Date	Before score	After score	Gain score

Total gain score _____

Calm Body, Clear Mind Data Record

Student _____ **Date** _____

For each Calm Body, Clear Mind situation, give the answer the student circled a value based on the following scale.

much better	better	slightly better	the same	worse
5	4	3	2	1

➤ Note the dates between which the student filled out cue sheets.

➤ Add the numeric values corresponding to the student's circled responses, and write this sum in the column for total score.

➤ Write the number of situations the student recorded under total number of situations (omit unused items).

➤ Compute the rate by dividing the total score by the total number of situations. The rate will give you a comparable score irrespective of the number of items rated.

➤ To compute the average rate, sum all numbers in the rate column and divide by the total number of figures you added in this column.

Dates (from____ to ____)	Total score	Total no. of situations	Rate

Dates (from_____ to _____)	Total score	Total no. of situations	Rate

Calm Body, Clear Mind Data Record, page 2

Average rate _____

Calming Actions Data Record

Student _____ **Date** _____

For each Calming Action situation, give the answer the student circled a value based on the following scale.

much better	better	slightly better	the same	worse
5	4	3	2	1

➤ Note the dates between which the student filled out cue sheets.

➤ For each time period, sum the scores separately for each Calming Action. Write this number in the column for total score under the respective Calming Action.

➤ Write the number of times each type of Calming Action was used during that period under the column for times used.

➤ To arrive at a rate, divide the total score by the number of times used.

➤ Compute the average rate for each Calming Action by summing the numbers in the rate column, then dividing by the total number of figures you added in this column.

Let Feelings Out

Dates (from_____ to _____)	Total score	Times used	Rate

Average rate _____

Talk about Feelings

Dates (from_____ to _____)	Total score	Times used	Rate

Average rate _____

Exercise

Dates (from____ to ____)	Total score	Times used	Rate

Average rate _____

Rest

Dates (from____ to ____)	Total score	Times used	Rate

Average rate _____

Use Distraction

Dates (from____ to ____)	Total score	Times used	Rate

Average rate _____

Calming Actions Data Record, page 2

Relaxation Bingo and Stress Management Crossword Puzzle Scoring Formulas

Student _____ **Date** _____

Relaxation Bingo

_____ (score) × 100 = _____ (percentage correct)
25

Compute the score by adding the number of blank spaces on the bingo items on page 56 of the Student Manual. This is the number the student answered correctly. Compute the percentage correct by dividing that number by 25, then multiplying by 100.

Student _____ **Date** _____

Stress Management Crossword Puzzle

_____ (score) × 100 = _____ (percentage correct)
23

Count the number of correct items on page 61 of the Student Manual to obtain the score. Divide this number by 23 and multiply by 100 to obtain the percentage correct.

About the Author

Diane de Anda, Ph.D., is an associate professor in the Department of Social Welfare at the UCLA School of Public Policy and Social Research. She is editor of the *Journal of Ethnic and Cultural Diversity in Social Work* and serves on the editorial boards of other scholarly journals. Dr. de Anda is the editor of the book *Controversial Issues in Multiculturalism and Violence: Diverse Populations and Communities* and has published numerous articles in scholarly journals on issues related to adolescent development and special problems of adolescent populations, such as stress and coping, violence prevention, and adolescent pregnancy, particularly with Latino and multicultural youth. She authored the entry "Adolescents" in the last two editions of the *Encyclopedia of Social Work.*

Dr. de Anda has been active for over 25 years in community agencies and foundations focused on service to youth, serving as an advisory committee member for the California Wellness Foundation's Pregnancy Prevention Initiative and conducting evaluations for intervention programs in a variety of community agencies. She is the author of *Project Peace,* a violence prevention program in which over 40,000 youth in several school districts have participated, as well as three books for young readers featuring Latino families: *The Ice Dove and Other Stories, The Immortal Rooster and Other Stories,* and *Dancing Miranda.*

Dr. de Anda received her bachelor's degree in history and a secondary teaching credential from Mount St. Mary's College, in Los Angeles, her master's in social welfare and pupil personnel services credential from the University of California at Berkeley, and her Ph.D. in education from UCLA. Over the years, she has worked with adolescent populations as a junior high school teacher, school social worker, and researcher. As an educator of social work practitioners who deal with youth and their families, she has, with her graduate students, pilot tested the program described in this guide over a number of years with a variety of multicultural youth groups at the middle and high school levels.